# MYTHOPOESIS

*and the*

# MODERN WORLD

M. ALAN KAZLEV

978-0-6452126-0-0

*Mythopoesis and the Modern World*

M. Alan Kazlev

Thema Classification: JBGB (Myths & Legends), DSBJ (Literary Studies), QRVK2 , VXW (Mysticism), ATMN (Film/Television Genres).

MANTICORE PRESS
WWW.MANTICORE.PRESS

# CONTENTS

## PREFACE

first wrote this essay in 2008 or thereabouts. Recently I decided to add additional material, especially on Jung, archetypes, tropes, and the nature of the Imaginal World. I also deleted several diagrams that pertain more to general metaphysics rather than to story-telling. However, all of the material relevant to story-telling has been retained.

# 1. INTRODUCTION

The topic of this essay is *mythopoesis*, a word I have adopted from Hellenistic Greek and which means "myth-making." *Mythopoeia* was used by the English linguist and fantasy author J. R. R. Tolkien in the 1930s and by others to refer to a genre that integrates traditional mythological themes and archetypes into contemporary fiction. Myth-making could be considered the highest form of that shared human pastime, story-telling. Many examples in popular culture, such as genre novels, television, cinema, comic books, and computer games, are able to incorporate classical Mythic archetypes, which have been re-shaped according to the understanding and worldview of contemporary authors and readers.

Proper consideration of this subject involves a review of ancient and modern art, poetry, comparative mythology, contemporary literature, critical film studies, music of every type and genre, dance (whether traditional, sacred, or modern), sculpture, architecture, the history of ideas, and more. Unfortunately, my knowledge of some of these subjects is limited. Nevertheless, as limited as such works may be, examining them can still be useful as indicators of predominant mythic trends and the interplay of popular culture and mass media. Emphasis is placed on the distinction between mundane and ego-based and Transpersonal/Mythic/sacred story-telling, with particular reference to my favorite genre, Fantastical Fiction and Sci-Fi. Themes of myth-making considered in a contemporary milieu include Otherworldliness, the Hero's Journey, the Encounter with the Other, Apocalypse, and Transcendence.

The thesis presented in this essay is as follows.

Everyday consciousness exists at the junction of two vast worlds or realities. These are the external world or physical universe known to science and empirical observation, and the inner world as described in myth, art, imagination, and phenomenology in general.

There are also other worlds or realities, such as dreams, the paranormal, psychedelic states, mystical states, etc. But to keep things simple, only these two, the outer and the inner, will be described in detail here.[1]

Consciousness itself is, in its essence, transcendental. It is the infinite field within which the experiences of the outer and the inner worlds arise and pass away. Pure consciousness in itself is untouched by these experiences. It is the witness, the Self or Atman of Vedanta philosophy, the Original mind of Mahayana and Tantric Buddhism.

By existing in and as a finite body, and interacting with the inner and outer worlds, consciousness takes on the form of an Ego, a relative "I" or self. The nature and dynamics of the Ego and its relation to the psyche as a whole is the

---

[1] These topics are explored in much more detail in my upcoming *Kheper Book of Gnosis*.

topic of psychology, particularly the psychology of Freud (emphasizes more the personal unconscious more) and Jung (who refers to the Ego in relation to the collective unconscious), and will not be explored here.

The premise of consciousness and Ego bridging two worlds implies that the inner world is not just an epiphenomenon of the brain, but as vast and autonomous as the outer world. I refer to this as — using the terminology of esotericist scholar Henry Corbin — an *Imaginal World*, which is the intermediate or transitional reality between the mundane or everyday reality on the one hand, and spiritual, noetic, and transcendent reality or realities on the other. It is suggested that myths and myth-making, rather than being *nothing but* subjective fantasies, are actually anthropomorphic (individual or collective fantasy projection) representations of this Imaginal reality. Just as rational consciousness and empiricism allows us to access the material reality (e.g., academic and scientific method), true imagination enables us to access the Imaginal. Here I must also distinguish between "fantasy" as a narcissistic wish-fulfillment activity of the profane ego and "fantasy" as a literary genre emphasizing magic and over technology, and at its best portraying Imaginal realities in an anthropomorphic mythopoetic guise. Hopefully, the context of the text will show which of these two totally unrelated definitions is meant.

## 2. IMAGINATION AND REASON

ythopoesis is the creation of Myth by means of Imagination.

In creating narratives (stories, explanations) by which reality can be understood, human beings have generally resorted to two approaches. These are Imagination and Reason (or Rationalism). These can also be referred to in terms of partially overlapping but not always synonymous polarities such as *mythos* and *logos*,[2] subjective and objective, dream and waking, magic

---

[2] The Greeks did not seem to make an opposing pair out of these two terms, and hence used them in a somewhat different sense to the contemporary turn of the 21st century usage. Regarding the latter, a google search will bring up numerous hits, in which luminaries like C. G. Jung and Karen Armstrong feature strongly. Regarding the former, see, for example, Walter A. Shelburne, *Mythos and Logos in the Thought of Carl Jung: The Theory of the Collective Unconscious in Scientific Perspective*, SUNY 1988. Regarding the latter, in an interview by *The Wall Street Journal* with Karen Armstrong and Richard Dawkins, each was asked, "Where does evolution leave God?" Dawkins states that evolution makes God redundant, although Teilhard de Chardin would beg to differ! While I have great admiration for Richard Dawkins, he is using a "straw man" argument. These comments only apply to the concept of a very literalist and anthropomorphic external deity that no-one outside fundamentalism would accept. This is not to deny that such fundamentalism does include a huge percentage of the Earth's population. Armstrong's definition is more nuanced, and

or religion and science, arts and sciences.[3] Note that mythos here is unrelated to mythos in the context of a self-contained religious or secular universe. The plural of mythos in this latter definition is mythoi.

refers instead to the two paths of finding truth which she calls mythos and logos. Logos or reason deals with external reality, and mythos — represented by Greek myths — were an early form of psychology. See the summary at The Hannibal Blog – Mythos and logos: Armstrong v Dawkins (22 Sep 2009) http://andreaskluth.org/2009/09/22/mythos-and-logos-armstrong-v-dawkins. While Mythos and Logos may be used to refer to the culture war between religion and secularism, for example, the war between Islamic extremism and Secular West (see for example "Mythos vs Logos – Islamic literalism (opium resurgence) history of conflict in Afghanistan" http://www.unique-design.net/library/mythos.html. This is only one rather extreme illustration, and ignores the fact that the West has its own mythos too. I find Professor Armstrong's views here are very much in accordance with mine, except that I extend mythos beyond merely psychology to Jungian, Corbinist, and archetypal dimensions. Note that the word mythos can also be used to refer to any individual mythopoetic world or framework. For example the "Cthulhu mythos" of Imaginal horror writer H. P. Lovecraft.

[3] For more on these sorts of correspondences, see Stan Gooch, *Total Man*, Abacus, 1972. See, for example, the list of correspondences on pp.82-3, which I reposted at http://malankazlev.com/kheper/topics/Gooch/Total_Man.html. Gooch's work exerted a very big influence on me back in 1980 and thereabouts. However, I find his physicalist explanations rather limited, and ignore these when studying his work (other grand synthesis writers like Jung and Wilber have similar problems). Interestingly, Gooch rejects Sperry's split brain research. However, there is absolutely no scientific evidence in favor of his own theory that "System B" (the Imagination pole) is located in the Cerebellum, which is actually associated with motor reflexes).

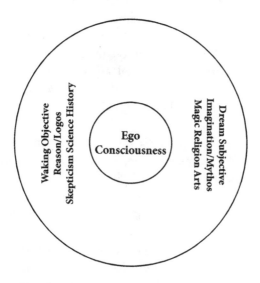

*Fig.1* The fundamental polarity of the human psyche. The ego consciousness can orientate itself to either the inner, subjective, imagination or "mythos", or the outer, objective, skeptical reason or "logos."

Imagination here means the world or realm of story-telling, dreams, fantasy, meaning, and archetype. Imagination can, in turn, be divided into a "light" and "dark" aspect, which can be called Apollonian and Dionysian.[4] However, I have not explored this topic sufficiently to comment further here.

---

[4] Friedrich Nietzsche, *The Birth of Tragedy from the Spirit of Music.* The Wikipedia page on "Apollonian and Dionysian" includes a list of correspondences; however the Apollonian polarity includes attributes of both Imagination and Reason, in other words, there are two types of Imagination. This fits in with Stan Gooch's b1 and b2 faculties.

It is essential to distinguish between imagination as trivial, narcissistic fantasies, daydreams, and various movements of the lower desire nature (what Sri Aurobindo calls the "vital being"[5]) and imagination in its higher and more creative, intuitive inspirational aspects. For the sake of convenience, the adjectives *Egoic* and *Mythic* are used to refer to lower and higher imagination.

Here, the Egoic represents the personal element of the psyche and the imagination, and the Mythic and the Transpersonal.

These categories can be supplemented with those of the more evocative (because of its religious nuances) terminology used by Romanian religious scholar Mircea Eliade: *profane* and *sacred*.[6] Hence there is an inferior, self-indulgent, profane (non-mystical) imagination and a higher, transcendent, mystical, sacred, transpersonal, and mythopoetic imagination.

I should emphasize here that sacred and profane are used not in a literalist religious or supernaturalist way but to highlight a particular polarity of consciousness. By "sacred," I mean anything numinous,[7] uplifting,

---

[5] Sri Aurobindo, *Letters on Yoga*, vol. I pp.334ff. More technically, it is the outer vital that is being referred to here, especially its mental expressions in the "mental vital" or "vital mind", not the inner vital, which is a source of esoteric and occult power, and an essential element of any spiritual practice.

[6] See Eliade's *The Sacred and the Profane: The Nature of Religion* (trans. Willard R. Trask), Harper Torchbooks, New York, 1961 and other works.

[7] Numinous is one of those intriguing words I picked up when first reading Jung. The Latin word *numen* means "presence"and is used to refer to the presence or sense of the sacred that comes from a deity or

wondrous, awe-inspiring, magical, and miraculous; by profane, the opposite.

While Eliade did not seem to specifically link imagination and sacred together, his friend and colleague at Eranos (an annual discussion group dedicated to the study of psychology, religion, philosophy, and spirituality), Henry Corbin certainly did, in the context of what he calls the Imaginal World. Corbin's insights in this regard are the source of inspiration for the present essay, even if I am sure he would not agree with some of my premises.

Both lower and higher imagination are found in popular culture and story-telling, most often intermixed and merged with the other. But what I here call the Egoic or profane imagination can only create degrading, one-dimensional characterizations which appeal to the lower aspects of the ego nature. Whereas Mythic or sacred imagination has true inspirational and initiatory power, which enables it to construct heroic archetypes and authentic mythoi (inspirational or imagined universes). In this way, story-telling, which is almost always grounded in fantasies of Egoic wish-fulfillment and Shadow and Anima/Animus projection (to use Jungian terminology), rises above the banal since it can access the sacred transpersonal, mythopoetic dimension, and thus serves as a path of spiritual transcendence, and even self-initiation.

---

a spirit in places and objects. The word was popularized by German theologian Rudolf Otto in his highly influential text *The Idea of the Holy* (published in 1917 as *Das Heilige – Über das Irrationale in der Idee des Göttlichen und sein Verhältnis zum Rationalen* (*The Holy – On the Irrational in the Idea of the Divine and its Relation to the Rational*).

The opposite pole to imagination with its lower and higher nature is the rational or conceptual mind, facts, theory, understanding, explanations, method, cause, and effect (whether on the metaphysical or the pragmatic sphere). Because "Reason" is often also used, especially in philosophy, to refer to the higher faculties of the mind, an alternative term, "skepticism," may be used, or even better, the two together, Skeptical Reason. Technically speaking, this is also "profane" because it is not of the nature of the mystical or sacred. But this is profane in a very different, totally neutral context. Hence I would prefer to use the word *mundane*, meaning "of the world," to refer to the skeptical, rational, or empirical approach and facts rather than meaning. But I would also use mundane to refer to any ordinary consensus reality that does not consider transpersonal and transcendent dimensions.

Although when taken to extremes, skepticism can lead to a stultifying reductionism or "reign of quantity,"[8] this is not authentic skepticism, any more than literalist fundamentalism is genuine religion. In its true sense, skepticism does not mean nihilism; it simply means rejecting those premises and realities that cannot be confirmed empirically. Without skepticism, science would be impossible because there would be no way to distinguish valid empirical realities from subjective fantasies. Skepticism should also not be confused with blanket denial. Denialism, whether in the materialistic and

---

[8] The phrase was coined by the French esotericist, Sufism convert, and founder of the Traditionalist movement, René Guénon, in his work *The Reign of Quantity and the Signs of the Times*. (first published in French in 1945). The Austrian Christian-Rosicrucian theosophist and clairvoyant Rudolf Steiner said something basically similar with his description of Ahriman, the cosmic spirit that draws human consciousness away from the Spiritual dimension and into materialism.

reductionistic context of the denial of all transcendental realities or in the pseudoscientific or conspiracy theory context[9] of denial of anthropogenic climate change, biological evolution, or the moon landings, has nothing to do with real science. Rationalism, not as a school of philosophy but in the colloquial sense, can be used as a synonym for Reason in skeptical science (hence we live in a scientific "age of rationalism").

So science, history, facts, and rationalism, are mundane, but they are not necessarily profane. Einstein, for example, was an empiricist and a Spinozan pantheist who rejected the idea of a supernatural God yet still spoke of a sense of wonder regarding the cosmos.[10] This is undoubtedly the cosmos as sacred, even in its most material form. Moreover, even history and evolution may constitute

---

[9] Special Report: Denial, in *New Scientist*, vol 206 mo. 2760 (15 May 2010) pp.35-45.

[10] According to English environmental writer and founder of the World Pantheist Movement Paul Harrison (see "Einstein, pantheist – A history of pantheism and scientific pantheism" http://www.pantheism.net/paul/einstein.htm ) "Einstein always said that he was a deeply religious man, and his religion informed his science. He rejected the conventional image of God as a personal being, concerned about our individual lives, judging us when we die, intervening in the laws he himself had created to cause miracles, answer prayers and so on. Einstein did not believe in a soul separate from the body, nor in an afterlife of any kind. ... But he was also struck by the radiant beauty, the harmony, the structure of the universe as it was accessible to reason and science. In describing these factors he sometimes uses the word God, and sometimes refers to a divine reason, spirit, or intelligence. He never suggests that this reason or spirit transcends the world – so in that sense he is a clear pantheist and not a panentheist." A great admirer of the 17th century Jewish Dutch philosopher, rationalist, and pantheist Baruch Spinoza, Einstein once famously replied, when asked if he believed in God, "I believe in Spinoza's God who reveals himself in the orderly harmony of what exists, not in a God who concerns himself with fates and actions of human beings."

the sacred unfolding of the Divine on both an individual and cosmological scale, as independently explained by both Sri Aurobindo in an Eastern context and Pierre Teilhard de Chardin in a European context.[11] This is why I reserve "profane" for the selfish ego and its self-gratifying projections and wish-fulfillment fantasies, and "mundane" for the material universe of time and space, as well as human socio-cultural history and individual personal history.

Although the association of terms like ego with profane may imply a sort of religious moralism, due to the misuse of the word ego by pop gurus and fake enlightened teachers who are concerned with "destroying the ego" of their followers (while carefully ignoring their own (Jesus' saying regarding the mote and the beam is particularly appropriate in such instances), that does not mean that the ego in itself is evil. Instead, it is a necessary stage that consciousness has to go through. For if it is to realize its individuality and not be consumed by the Whole, it is essential for consciousness, at least for a while, to adopt the false opinion that the entire cosmos revolves around itself.

This dynamic, which is profoundly analyzed in Eastern Vedanta and yoga psychology in terms of its various aspects of *klesha* (taint), *mala* (dross), *kanchuka* (covering), and *koshas* (veil) (to go into this fascinating topic would take too long here), is what maintains separative existence and ignorance by the consciousness of

---

[11] Sri Aurobindo, *The Life Divine*; Teilhard de Chardin, *The Phenomenon of Man*. On the parallels between the philosophies of these two great visionaries, neither of which knew the other, see R. C. Zaehner (1971) *Evolution in Religion: A Study in Sri Aurobindo and Pierre Teilhard de Chardin*, Clarendon Press, Oxford; Beatrice Bruteau (1974), *Evolution Towards Divinity* (Theosophical Publishing House, Wheaton, Ill); David M. Brookman, *Teilhard and Aurobindo: A Study in Religious Complementarity*, Mayur Publications, 1988; and many other works.

its true nature. Through natural spiritual growth and self-development, and *never* through abusive manipulations of an external ignorant so-called "guru," the self-obsessed ego gradually drops away, and consciousness realizes its true nature as being of the Supreme.

Both profane and mundane pertain to the *exoteric* or external reality, whether it be the external material world or the subjective ego. This is the opposite of the inner, spiritual, gnostic,[12] esoteric[13] reality, which transcends the personal ego and everyday consciousness.

---

[12] *Gnosis* was originally the common Greek noun for knowledge, but in various Hellenistic religions and philosophies came to mean higher or spiritual knowledge. For example, the dualistic Judaic and Christian mystery religions of the late Hellenistic period were called Gnosis or Gnosticism because of their emphasis on such gnosis and its application as transcendent or saving knowledge. See e.g. Hans Jonas, *The Gnostic Religion* (Boston: Beacon, 1963) and many later works by other authors, James M. Robinson, ed. *The Nag Hammadi Library in English*. 3d ed. San Francisco: Harper & Row, 1988. Equivalent terms in Vedanta, Jainism, Buddhism, and Sufism, include *jnana, kevala, prajna, sambodhi, atma-vidya, satori, tasawwuf, irfan*, and *ma'rifah*. All refer to a more profound way of knowing, a knowing that both reveals eternal truths and creates new insights and revelations, that transforms the individual consciousness and allows one to pass beyond the limitation of the finite self, the little "I" or ego.

[13] Originally, esotericism referred to the secret or inner, that is, "esoteric," teachings and techniques revealed only to initiates in secret societies or to those initiated into the mysteries, such as those of Ancient Egypt, or Pythagoreanism, as opposed to the outer or "exoteric". The word is traditionally attributed to Aristotle, although the oldest known occurrence of the Greek adjective *esôterikos* is Lucian of Samosata, in the 2nd century C.E. It reappeared in the West in the early 18th century. In the 19th century Anglo-French occult revival, "Esotericism", like "Occultism", came to mean the science of hidden or subtle realities that lie beyond or behind the surfaces. This definition dates specifically to the work of Eliphas Levi and A. P. Sinnett, but was only really popularized in the 20th century by post-theosophist Alice Bailey with a series of books such as *Esoteric Astrology* and *Esoteric Christianity*. It is used here in the colloquial New Age sense.

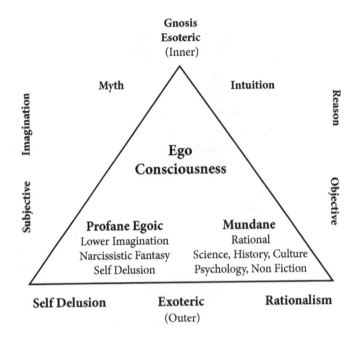

*Fig.2* The dual polarity of consciousness. This diagram differs from fig.1 in that it adds the polarity of exoteric and esoteric to that of subjective and objective. Outer or exoteric reality (*bottom*) may be mundane and rational (objective and factual) or profane and Egoic (subjective and self-delusional). Inner or esoteric reality (*top*) is spiritual, imaginal, and gnostic. Imagination (*left*) may be lower (subjective wish-fulfillment) or higher (mythic). One may also similarly contrast a higher intuitive Reason with a lower rationalism (*right*). Note that inner and subjective, as defined here, are not the same.

Physically, historically — that is, in the mundane world, the plane of being that is opposite yet complementary to the Imaginal — no creative act occurs in a vacuum (metaphorically speaking. One may envisage the creative processes of nature in the vacuum of outer space).

Individual mythopoesis still involves influences from society and culture as a whole. Although the noumenal or archetypal foundation of myth derives from the Imaginal World, or even from the Noetic, which is the reality beyond the Imaginal, it is experienced personally and subjectively through the individual consciousness. There is also the collective role that myth (whether as religious dogma or more spontaneous creative story-telling) plays in the society and culture as a whole.

Two very different but complementary representations here are Jung's model of the Ego and the Psyche, and integral American philosopher Ken Wilber's "AQAL" diagram, featuring a double polarity.

# 3. C. G. JUNG AND THE NATURE OF THE PSYCHE

Carl Gustav Jung was a Swiss psychologist and student of Freud, a member of the psychoanalytic school in Vienna, who was dissatisfied with Freud's limited approach.

Jung became fascinated by the way specific images and symbols appeared in the dreams and spontaneous fantasies of his patients. On researching these, he would discover the very same myths and symbols in ancient classical works or obscure alchemical texts.

He concluded that there is a common source of myth and meaning that is universal and appears regardless of culture or historical period. He called this the Collective Unconscious, which he contrasted with Freud's personal or individual unconscious. The personalities that inhabit the Collective Unconscious he referred to as Archetypes and stated these were the same as what in previous times were called gods. These same archetypes appear time and again, in stories and legends, in different guises but always with the same underlying structure.

For Jung, these archetypes are innate universal prototypes of ideas that tend to form mythological images or motifs and are potent symbols of transformation.

The major archetypes he referred to are the Anima/
Animus, the Self, the Shadow, the Wise Old Man, the
Child, the Mother, and the Maiden. These archetypes
occur even in the symbolism of medieval alchemists and
in the fantasies of schizophrenic patients.

In the Jungian model of the psyche, the Ego constitutes the
outer layer of the psyche, in contrast to the personal and the
collective Unconscious. It possesses the four functions of
thinking and feeling, and sensation and intuition.[14] At any
one time, one of each pair is always conscious, the other
unconscious. Thought and sentiment are both "rational"
because they evaluate, even if one is more "head" or fact-
centered and the other more "heart" or value-centered.
In contrast, sensation and intuition are "irrational"
because they perceive spontaneous outer (senses) or inner
(unconscious or psychic) realities. This has nothing to do
with the Platonic distinction between the Rational (mental)
and the Irrational (*thymos* and *epithymia*) soul.

When the evaluating (thinking and feeling) function is
paired with the sensory function, the Ego can be directed
to the everyday, mundane, outer, pragmatic, empirical
world of facts.

---

[14] C. G. Jung, *Psychological Types*, Collected Works, Volume 6, Princeton,
N.J.: Princeton University Press, (1971). The four Ego faculties can
automatically be associated with the four elements of Greek science and
Western esotericism: sensation is earth, feeling is water, thinking is air,
and intuition is fire. Although it is tempting to associate thinking and
sensation with the empirical world and science, this is not necessarily
the case regarding sensation, as many scientists are highly intuitive. But
in general intuition and mythopoesis would seem to go together, in that
any mythopoesis must be an intuitive act of creation. An interesting
dynamic Jung observed regarding these faculties is that when one pole
is conscious (the Ego), the other is unconscious (the Shadow). This
probably applies to the psyche and consciousness in general.

For convenience, the Ego directed outwards, using thinking or feeling to test and interact with objective reality, is referred to as Logos.

Conversely, when an evaluating function is paired with the intuition function, it can be directed to the inner, daydreaming, fantastical world of imagination. The Ego directed inwards and using the imagination to create and participate in its reality is Mythos.

As in Freudian psychology, the Jungian Ego has to mediate between the inner (unconscious psyche) and the outer (social and empirical) realities. The partial equivalent of the Freudian superego or conscience would be the "mask" or social convention the Ego puts on in order to interact with the social world, called the Persona.

In the opposite direction, are the repressed, and therefore unconscious, aspects of the ego-personality he referred to as the Shadow. In part equivalent to the Freudian Id or It, this contains all those elements the Ego does not wish to confront or acknowledge and is, therefore, the individual personification of evil within the psyche.

Finally, within the Collective Unconscious, the Self (with a capital "S") is a hidden counter Ego that regulates the psyche and the unconscious as a whole, just as the Ego controls the conscious personality. The Self is represented by images of the sacred, for example, figures like Christ or Buddha. It is also the central archetype in the individuation process, representing the union of opposites, the symbol of totality, often represented by *mandalas*.

Jung noticed meaningful coincidences which could not be causally explained. He related one example of a young female patient who had a dream in which she was given a golden scarab. As she was telling this dream to Jung, he heard a gentle tapping against the window behind him. He turned and opened the window, and in flew a scarab beetle. The coincidence was so extraordinary it broke through the rationalism and resistance of her *Animus* so the process of transformation could begin.[15]

On the basis of such experiences, Jung came to understand that, contrary to the reductionist-materialist worldview he was brought up in, the unconscious psyche appeared to have a supra-subjectivity independent of the ordinary causality. With the help of the Austrian quantum physicist Wolfgang Pauli, he tied this in with modern physics, referred to this acausality as Synchronicity.

For Jung, then archetypes have a dual nature, existing both in the psyche and the world. This latter (synchronistic) aspect of the archetype he refers to as "psychoid."[16]

---

[15] C. G. Jung, *Synchronicity: An Acausal Connecting Principle*. (From Vol. 8. of the Collected Works of C. G. Jung), Translated by R. F. C. Hull. Princeton University Press, 1983, 2010 pp.22f, p.110.

[16] *Ibid* pp.20, 89, 97.

## 4. KEN WILBER AND THE ALL QUADRANTS CLASSIFICATION

In Wilber's model, there is the distinction between "interior" and "exterior" on the one hand – equivalent to Mythos and Logo, Imagination and Reason/Empiricism, and individual and collective on the other. So the interior-individual is individual consciousness, the exterior-individual is behavior, the interior-collective is culture (which is the realm of language, myth, and so on; here, the arts and sciences represent the imagination-reason polarity), and the exterior-collective is society.[17] Because myth, by its very nature, operates on the collective level of cultures, societies, religions, and worldviews as a whole, to understand myth, it is necessary to consider the collective, socio-cultural sphere.

Wilber's system is a rationalistic taxonomy (categorizing states of consciousness and fields of knowledge in terms of

---

[17] The AQAL diagram and its explanation has been repeated many times in Wilber's own books and those of his students, as well as on-line. My synopsis is intentionally simplistic; for a more detailed account see e.g. Ken Wilber, *A Brief History of Everything*, Boston and London: Shambhala. ch. 5-7; *Integral Spirituality: A Startling New Role for Religion in the Modern and Postmodern World*, Integral Books, 2006 pp. 20ff., and Sean Esbjorn-Hargens, An Overview of Integral Theory : An All-Inclusive Framework for the 21st Century Integral Life <http://integrallife.com/node/37539>.

quadrants, zones, lines of development, states, and stages) rather than a psychological phenomenology like Jung, which pertains to the mundane world only. Although he and his followers claim to also incorporate subtle and causal states of existence,[18] these feel like they're tacked on rather than part of a single holistic model of consciousness. But while less than satisfactory from a gnostic, esoteric, and metaphysical perspective, it still provides some valuable insights regarding the mundane world, especially the socio-cultural dimension.

Wilber's Integral Theory understands culture and socio-cultural worldviews or belief systems as belonging to the shared or collective subjective (or "intersubjective"; I use this word in brackets because there are several definitions[19]) quadrant, which includes words, ideas, and so on, and society to the collective objective, which includes physical people, structures, artifacts, and systems. I would further divide the individual subjective into imagination and reason (section 2) and the "intersubjective" likewise into religion/myth and science/philosophy. Myth and religion pertain to the imagination pole of the "intersubjective," and secular knowledge, philosophy, and the hard and soft sciences to the rational pole.

---

[18] Ken Wilber, "Toward A Comprehensive Theory of Subtle Energies", Excerpt G, <http://wilber.shambhala.com/html/books/kosmos/excerptG/part1.cfm/> For a critique, see Frank Visser, Reflections on "Subtle energy" <http://www.integralworld.net/visser3.html>.

[19] Christian de Quincey, Intersubjectivity: Exploring Consciousness from the Second-Person Perspective. <http://cognet.mit.edu/posters/TUCSON3/deQuincey.html> (Retrieved 28 May 2010).

**Upper-Left Quadrant**
Interior - Individual
Intentional

| | |
|---|---|
| Subtle Body | |
| Occult & Transpersonal | |
| Experiences | |

| | |
|---|---|
| Imagination | Reason |
| Fantasy | Facts, Knowledge, |
| Dreams | Understanding |
| Meaning | Regarding "real life" |

**Upper-Right Quadrant**
Interior - Individual
Intentional

**Imaginal World**
**(Objective)**

| | |
|---|---|
| Myth | Science |
| Religion | Philosophy |
| Art | Modernity |

**Material World**
**(Objective)**

"Collective Unconscious"
(Jung) and "Spiritual
Heirarchies"
(Steiner)

**Lower-Right Quadrant**
Exterior - Collective
Social (Systems)

Interior-Collective
Cultural
**Lower-Left Quadrant**

*Fig.3.* Extending Wilber's four quadrants to include the Imaginal (left) and the Mundane (right) world. Wilber's Integral Theory ("Integral Post-Metaphysics") is perspectival only (Wilber, *Integral Spirituality*, pp. 42ff.), whereas I prefer critical realism regarding the Mundane material-physical world and metaphysics and essentialism regarding the Imaginal. This diagram can be considered an elaboration of fig. 1. It includes the Mundane material world (right) and the sacred Imaginal World (left), but not the Egoic sphere, which would constitute a third axis (see fig.2). Both the Mundane and the Imaginal Worlds are equally "objective" in that both constitute realities that are not limited by subjective preconceptions or psychological factors. However, Imaginal objectivity requires metaphysics and gnosis to be understood and appreciated, whereas Mundane objectivity is easily accessed through rationalism and empirical observation.

A complete understanding of mythopoesis has to include both the vertical spectrum of Mundane, Imaginal, and Noetic (and also physical, emotional, and mental states of consciousness within the Mundane and Imaginal), a horizontal polarity of reason/material world and imagination/Imaginal World, the socio-cultural polarity of individual and collective, the psychological polarity of Egoic/mundane-personality and Mythic/transpersonal, and the mystical or spiritual polarity of sacred and profane. Because of the fractal nature of reality, in which there are worlds within worlds and sub-degrees of consciousness within degrees, this psychology is also included within esoteric cosmology and vice-versa.

## 5. MYTH AND FAERIE

Joseph Campbell was an American scholar of comparative mythology and religion and the author of classic works on this subject such as the four-volume *The Masks of God* (1959-68), a comprehensive review of world mythology, and *The Hero with a Thousand Faces* (1949), in which he discusses the hero's journey as described in common in world mythologies (hence the term monomyth). Campbell studied how Freud and Jung used myth in psychology, and although he never met Jung, he was greatly influenced by him. Campbell's conception of myth was based on Jung's method of dream interpretation, which revolves around the use of symbols.

*The Hero with a Thousand Faces* was one of the influences George Lucas used, but certainly not the only one, when he created *Star Wars* (1977), arguably, along with Tolkien's *Lord of the Rings*, the most influential work of 20th century mythopoesis. Lucas' talent lay in the way he could splice together a huge range of movies and source materials. He had already developed the basic story but used Campbell's work as a further guide.[20] Because of *Star*

---

[20] Forrest Wickman. *Star Wars is* a Postmodern Masterpiece – How George Lucas spliced together Westerns, *jidaigeki,* space adventure serials, fairy tales, dogfighting movies, and Casablanca to create

*Wars'* incredible success, *The Hero with a Thousand Faces* became a *de rigeur* textbook for aspiring screenwriters.

Campbell's mythography is perhaps more approachable than Jung's, and it is easy to see how Lucas could apply it to his work. Nevertheless, it's unnecessary to be familiar with Campbell or Jung, like Lucas or the Wachowskis (*The Matrix*), to write an archetypal story. The whole idea of the archetypes, and a universal Mythic consciousness, is that it's something that appears spontaneously. All one needs is inspiration. So the tackiest novels and movies can incorporate archetypal or mythic themes, even if they don't do it very well.

While conversely, a genius like J. R. R Tolkien didn't need to read his contemporaries, Jung or Campbell, at all because he went straight to the source like them.

Tolkien wasn't a non-fiction writer like Jung or Campbell, but his comprehensive world-building and story-telling of Middle Earth are the story-telling equivalent. And like Jung, he asserted a universal, objective source of myth and legend.

In his 1939 essay and lecture "*On Fairy Stories*," he refers to Faerie as both a fictitious realm and a transcendent realm, like the Jungian "The Collective Unconscious," from which Man derives his creativity. In his 1931 poem *Mythopoeia,* he explained and defended myth-making as a creative art about "fundamental things."[21]

Hollywood's first world-conquering collage. Slate, 13 December, 2015 <http://www.slate.com/articles/arts/cover_story/2015/12/star_wars_is_a_pastiche_how_george_lucas_combined_flash_gordon_westerns.html> (Retrieved 21 May 2021).

[21] Tolkien, J. R. R. 1964/2001, "Mythopoeia; The Homecoming of

The concept of Faerie also occurs in the Islamic world under the name of Jinn.[22] Best known in the West through sanitized cartoons like the magic genie of *Aladdin's Lamp*, Jinn are ubiquitous in Islamic myths, poetry, folklore, and literature. According to the Quran, God created two parallel species: man from clay and Jinn from smokeless fire.[23]

English writer Patrick Harpur refers to this as Daimonic Reality,[24] which is another way of understanding Jung's Collective Unconscious and the *Anima Mundi* or World Soul of Renaissance and Elizabethan philosophy (although going back to Plotinus). He includes such anomalous realities as the Loch Ness Monster, Big Foot, UFOs, crop circles, guardian angels, and visions of the Virgin Mary, all of which qualify as Fortean Phenomena (after American paranormal investigator Charles Fort[25]).

Beorhtnoth Beorhthelm's Son" in *Tree and Leaf*. New York and London: Harper Collins.

[22] Amira El-Zein, *Islam, Arabs, and the Intelligent World of the Jinn*, Syracuse University Press, 2009.

[23] For example verse 55: 15 (Quranic Arabic Corpus, <https://corpus.quran.com/translation.jsp?chapter=55&verse=15> (Retrieved 26 May 2021) and Al-Jinn, Wikipedia, edit of 21 January 2021.

[24] Patrick Harpur, *Daimonic Reality: A Field Guide to the Otherworld*, Pine Winds Press 1994, 2003.

[25] Charles Fort, *The Book of the Damned*, Ace Books, 1972, first published in 1919. This and subsequent books described scientific anomalies such as unexplained aerial phenomena (UFOs, long before 1947 when American aviator and businessman Kenneth Arnold reported nine unusual flying objects, which the press reported as "flying saucers"), rains of fish, frogs, and so on, teleportation, poltergeists, forbidden archeology, fairies. His work had a large influence on both speculative fiction (H. P. Lovecraft, Robert Heinlein, Alfred Bester, Philip K. Dick, Robert Anton Wilson, Stephen King, and many others, the New Age (Louis Pauwels and Jacques Bergier's

The contrast between rational Ego and daimonic Unconscious is ubiquitous. Variously called the Double, Doppelganger, Id, the Vital, and so on, and associated with folklore tales from both the East and West – such as *Rip van Winkle* and *Monkey's Journey to the West*.[26]

Jung, Campbell, and Tolkien are all saying we have an intrinsic psychological need to believe in and experience myth and magic in our lives; this is an inherent part of human nature. Jung points to the irrepressible nature of the archetype, which will take on the forms of modern-day life.[27]

---

*The Morning of the Magicians*), and paranormal researchers (Ivan T. Sanderson). The British monthly journal *Fortean Times* was first published in 1973 and is still going strong.

[26] Steven Guth, The Double, a new paradigm for understanding the human psyche, 2003 <http://malankazlev.com/kheper/topics/double/>.

[27] "Archetypes are complexes of experience that come upon us like fate, and their effects are felt in our most personal life. The Anima no longer crosses our path as a goddess, but, it may be, as an intimately personal misadventure, or perhaps as our best venture. When, for instance, a highly esteemed professor in his seventies abandons his family and runs off with a young red-headed actress, we know that the gods have claimed another victim." – Archetypes and the Collective Unconscious (1935). In Collected Works vol 9, Part 1: *The Archetypes and the Collective Unconscious*, paragraph 62.

## 6. RECAPITULATION

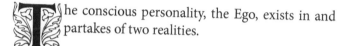The conscious personality, the Ego, exists in and partakes of two realities.

The physical reality is the external world of facts, which is experienced through the senses and understood through the rational mind, specifically the Thinking ego-function (or Thinking with Sensation as the secondary function), or what can be called Logos. Examples of this are science, technology, history, economics, statistics, analytical philosophy, and non-fiction.

And there is the psychological and psychic reality, the inner world of meaning, which is experienced through feelings and the imagination, and understood through the intuitive mind, specifically the Feeling, Intuitive, and Intuitive-Thinking ego-functions that can be called Mythos. Examples of this are myths, folklore, stories, religions, legends, music, art, and so on.

Religious concepts such as God do not describe a cosmological, metaphysical reality where an invisible anthropomorphic personality creator creates the universe, but are a projection of the inner reality upon the limited ego.

n, empiricism and
vidual polarity or

wo different realms.

spect, such as wish-
t religions, political
, blockbuster movies
story), and reality TV

And there is a larger, more epic, transpersonal and transcendent aspect, full of wonder, which provides meaning and purpose in life. Without it, everything would be empty and soulless, a colorless world of mere quantitative facts.

The Ego itself is typically limited to a mundane, everyday reality in which it is the center of personal existence. But, just as the mundane part of the Ego partakes of the external world and the small thoughts and desires of everyday life, the higher imagination can orientate that same Ego to the Transpersonal, to a universal inner world beyond its boundaries. This is variously called the Collective Unconscious, the Imaginal World, the Daimonic Reality, Myth, Legend, Fairie, the other world, etc.

This larger psychic world is the source of all myth-making, of mythopoesis. Myth, imagination, folklore, art, and stories all are the reworking of this inner, sacred, transpersonal reality in a way the ego-personality can understand and resonate with and, hopefully, find it uplifting.

## 7. THE IMAGINAL WORLD

The ordinary narcissistic imagination of the Ego cannot access this reality, being limited as it is to personal daydreams and wish-fulfillment fantasies. In other words, there is a universal world or plane of existence that corresponds to the individual imagination. Of course, mundane Egoic imagination cannot access this reality, as it is tied to personal fantasy and wish-fulfillment. It is, in other words, profane. But the transpersonal, inspirational, sacred imagination can access it. This universe of imagination is referred to as the Imaginal World.

The word Imaginal was coined by the French esotericist and academic Henry Corbin (1903-1978), who was professor of Islamic Studies at the Sorbonne in Paris, based on his studies of the teachings of Islamic esotericists such as Suhrawardi and ibn Arabi. Even though the Imaginal is the world of the imagination, it is not an imaginary world (using imaginary in the contemporary sense of the term). Corbin distinguishes between the modern skeptical mind and the spiritual imagination of esotericism (e.g., Ishraqism and Sufism). The latter can access the transitional reality between the material-physical and the transcendent spiritual, which he calls the Imaginal.[28]

---

[28] Henry Corbin, *Mundus Imaginalis, or the Imaginary and the*

Some analogies of the Imaginal in both other spiritual traditions and more recent accounts are the sidereal or astral spheres of Chaldean and Late Platonic occultism, which became the basis for Renaissance occultism, Paracelsianism, and some of Blavatsky's Theosophy, the *bardo* or intermediate state of Tibetan Buddhism, the various concepts of the subtle body in Tantra and Taoism,[29] the spirit world as described by Emmanuel Swedenborg, the astral plane of post-Blavatsky Theosophy[30] and similar accounts of the human aura in the New Age and Wellness movements,[31] and accounts of out of body experiences

*Imaginal*. in Leonard Fox transl. *Swedenborg and Esoteric Islam*. West Chester, PE: Swedenborg Foundation (1995). Although Corbin's Imaginal world technically corresponds to the worlds of *mithal* and *malakut* in Sufi cosmology, it also has a more phenomenological character that is not found in the traditional, stylized texts. As with other esoteric systems such as Kabbalah and Tantra, these themes are presented in a heavily formalized and premodern religious style that required personal instruction of a teacher or guru if they were to be comprehensible. In this regard, Corbin's familiarity with the philosophies of Heidegger and Jung enabled him to present these themes in a way that they could be understood by the intelligent layperson, without sacrificing the traditional esoteric insights the teachings contain.

[29] Simon Paul Cox, *A Genealogy of the Subtle Body*, Rice University Electronic Theses and Dissertations (2019) Diss., Rice University. <https://hdl. handle.net/1911/107458>.

[30] See, for example, C. W. Leadbeater, *Man Visible and Invisible*. London: Theosophical Publishing House, 1920, and many other works. A. E. Powell, *The Astral Body and Other Astral Phenomena*, Quest Books, The Theosophical Publishing House; Fourth Printing 1987 (first published 1927) brings together all the material by Leadbeater and Annie Besant on the Astral body and the Astral Plane. There are also his companion volumes on the Etheric body, the Mental body, and the Causal body.

[31] While there is a huge range of material published, almost all of it goes back to Barbara Ann Brennan, *Hands of Light: A Guide to Healing Through the Human Energy Field*, Bantam, 1987.

reported by Sylvan Muldoon and Hereward Carrington, Robert Monroe, Jurgen Ziewe, and many others.

But perhaps the best comparison of Imaginal is with the Collective Unconscious. Although Corbin developed many of his insights independently, he later became aware of and influenced by the work of Swiss psychologist C. G. Jung, which he encountered during his Eranos Period (1949 onwards). The two men became friends, and he extensively appropriated much of Jung's technical vocabulary.[32] Jung's observations[33] of mythic symbolism in his patients' dreams and spontaneous fantasies possessed the same symbols found in obscure mythological and alchemical texts, constituting empirical and phenomenological evidence for an Imaginal reality independent of individual consciousness. But even if Jung's psychological and biological explanations of myth and symbol and excessive psychological reductionism might disappoint the rigorous metaphysician or be unsatisfactory to the modern critical scholar of esotericism,[34] his detailed

---

[32] Wasserstrom, *Religion After Religion*. pp.186-7.

[33] Jung's books, such as *The Archetypes and the Collective Unconscious, Aion: Researches into the Phenomenology of the Self*, and his alchemical studies (all included in the Collected Works published Bollingen in Princeton and Routledge and Kegan Paul in London), while packed with fascinating material, are heavy going, and the beginner is better served by his primer *Man and His Symbols*, published in 1964, which he wrote with four of his students: Joseph L. Henderson, Marie-Louise von Franz, Aniela Jaffé, and Jolande Jacobi. Jung's studies in myth were further developed by James Hillman, Joseph Campbell, and others.

[34] Esoteric academic and YouTube educator Justin Sledge, for example, includes the "Spiritual/Psychology School of Interpretation" among the popular misconceptions of alchemy. Justin Sledge, Five Misconceptions about Alchemy, Esoterica, YouTube, 20 March 2020 <https://youtu.be/0JE7Xi72eVk>.

and profound observations and intuitions on the nature and phenomenology of myth are still essential for any comprehensive understanding. The best way to approach Jung is as a phenomenologist, essentially, as a scientist of the experiences of interior (Imaginal) worlds. Alternatively, one could interpret the Jungian Unconscious as those aspects of Imaginal reality that are accessible to the individual's consciousness and influences of the Imaginal that have been internalized and appropriated by the individual subconscious. This opens the way for a rich field of psychological and esoteric exploration, and the transdisciplinary union of the Jungian psychology (and hence also Transpersonal Psychology as defined by Stan Grof, Michael Washburn, and others[35]) on the one hand, and metaphysics, esotericism, and occultism on the other.

---

[35] See, for example, Stanislav Grof, *Realms of the Human Unconscious*, New York, NY: Viking, 1975, and *Beyond the Brain*, Albany, NY: State University of New York Press, 1985; Michael Washburn, *Transpersonal Psychology in Psychoanalytic Perspective*, Albany, NY: State University of New York Press, 1994 and *The Ego and the Dynamic Ground* (2d Ed.), Albany, NY: State University of New York Press, 1995. The non-hierarchical non-linear models of human development found in Transpersonal Psychology contrast with the linear developmental psychology model of Ken Wilber, who has dissociated himself from Transpersonal Psychology to establish his own field of Integral Theory (see for example his *Integral Psychology*, Boston: Shambala, 2000), and is highly critical of the Jungian approach (including his own early Jungian-influenced work), charging that it fails to distinguish between pre-rational (infantile) and trans-rational (mystical) states of development. In fact there is no contradiction, as Wilber is tracing the path of the Ego and its transcendence, whereas Transpersonal Psychology is concerned with transpersonal states (whether pre – or trans-rational) beyond the Ego. For a systems approach, and also applications in different traditional and contemporary contemplative and transformative teachings, see Charles T. Tart, *Transpersonal Psychologies*, New York: Harper & Row, 1975.

Corbin's "Imaginal" is used as a synonym for its Jungian equivalent, "Collective Unconscious." The difference is that the concept of the Imaginal emphasizes the objective, trans-individual nature of this reality. Although Imaginal themes and archetypes are found in and mediated by the Unconscious Psyche (and conversely, the Unconscious itself is also part of the Imaginal[36]), the Imaginal itself is just as real, just as cosmic, and just as objective as the physical world of space and time, energy and matter. Corbin emphasizes this, and so does Steiner, for whom thought and spiritual beings have an objective rather than subjective reality. As the American scholar of comparative religion Huston Smith explains in his concise but practical books *Forgotten Truth* and *Beyond the Postmodern Mind*, this is a universal or perennial[37] understanding that modernity and postmodernity have lost and needs to be regained.

---

[36] As shown by Mirra Alfassa (The Mother of the Sri Aurobindo Ashram)'s experiences of the vital, the subconscious, and conscious sleep (lucid dreaming, but far more advanced than the standard New Age variety; consider also Tibetan Dream Yoga); see numerous references in *Mother's Agenda*, edited by Satprem.

[37] By *perennialism* is meant the understanding that certain spiritual and metaphysical insights and realizations are universal; they are not dependent on socio-cultural or individual psychological factors, although they may be influenced by them. Perennialism, therefore, is the opposite of *postmodernism*. Here I am not talking about Postmodernism in film, art or architecture, but Deconstructionism, Contextualism, and a host of other schools. All of these make up an academic paradigm which states that all so-called metaphysical and transcendental experiences and realities are culturally and linguistically conditioned. For different examples of Perennialism, see Frithjof Schuon, *The Transcendent Unity of Religions*, 1984, Theosophical Publishing House, Wheaton, Ill. (with introduction by Huston Smith); Aldous Huxley, *The Perennial Philosophy*, Harper Colophon Books, Harper & Row, New York, 1970; and Robert Forman, (ed.) (1990). *The Problem of Pure Consciousness: Mysticism and Philosophy*, Oxford University Press.

But not, I would add, at the expense of the insights of modernity, which are just as valid and authentic, and need to be incorporated.

*Fig. 4. The Ancient of Days*, by William Blake, a vision of the Imaginal World. Originally published as the frontispiece to his 1794 work *Europe a Prophecy*, this was one of Blake's favorite themes, and many copies have survived.

The reference is to one of God's titles in the Book of Daniel; in Hebrew *Atik Yomin*. In the Jewish occult-mystical system of Kabbalah, Atik Yomin is the very first emanation of the Godhead, called *En Sof* (The Endless). As the highest of the Partzufim or "physiognomies" of God, pertaining to the uppermost degree of the highest of the created worlds, called Atzilut ("Emanation"). The equivalent to Atzilut in Neoplatonism (fig. 5) is the Nous or Divine Mind.

Blake's figure, however, refers not to the highest Godhead, the supreme creator being, but to a lesser entity, the demiurge, whom he calls Urizen. This powerful image shows the creator being crouching in a circular design with a cloud-like background. His outstretched hand holds a compass over the darker void below. This is the compass and set square of freemasonry, which was also the "Golden Compass" in the Philip Pullman Science Fantasy Series of the same name.

Blake's visionary artwork and poetry refers not to the highest noetic-divine realms but an intermediary, visionary region of deities and celestial forms, in other words, the Imaginal realm.

## 8. THE HIERARCHY OF BEING

The Imaginal universe needs to be understood not only in terms of Jung's archetypes but also in the context of "vertical" cosmology, based around the theme of emanation (outflowing or outpouring or radiating from an original Supreme Source) and a spectrum or gradation of being from Spirit to Matter.[38] Here we have the "Great Chain of Being," as described in various occult and esoteric cosmologies (Neoplatonism,

---

[38] Smith, Huston, *Forgotten Truth: The Primordial Tradition*, New York: Harper & Row 1977. Plotinus' *Enneads* represents the clearest exposition of this cosmology, but examples can be found in other traditions too, e.g. the Upanishads, Kabbalah, Tantra, and elsewhere. It is represented traditionally by the world axis and microcosmically by the Tantric *chakra* system and equivalent themes. Detailed descriptions are also found in the teachings of Shiv Dayal Singh *Sar Bachan* (Sant Mat/Radha Soami), Max Theon's Cosmic tradition (see the Kheper website <http://malankazlev.com/kheper/topics/Theon/index.html>, and my upcoming *Kheper Book of Gnosis*). However, not all esoteric metaphysics follows the same basic theme of physical, Imaginal, Noetic, and absolute reality. The various spiritual traditions and philosophies differ in details regarding the number and nature of the various hypostases or realities, as well as their relationship. For example, the Western emanation model that goes back to Neoplatonism has a single vertical sequence like the one described here, above (even more so in the case of subsequent developments like Kabbalah or Theosophy), whereas the Eastern nonduality teachings of Mahayana Buddhism, Advaita Vedanta, and Kashmir Shaivism have the Absolute including and identical to the other realities.

Ishraqism, Sufism, Kabbalah, Shaiva Siddhanta, Panchatantra, Sant Mat, Theosophy, etc.).

Perhaps the most systematic development of this theme can be found in the metaphysics of the 3rd century Hellenistic-Egyptian mystic Plotinus and his successors, referred to as Neoplatonism (a modern term, Plotinus and his school would have been considered Platonists).

Synthesizing Middle Platonism, Aristotelianism, and Stoicism, Plotinus developed an elegant philosophical-mystical system. His lectures were compiled by his student Porphyry as the *Enneads*, or "nines," so-called because each of the six books was arranged in nine parts and survive today in both the original and several translations.

The metaphysics of Neoplatonism is based on the emanation or outpouring of the universe from the One or Absolute Reality. The One first emanates the Divine Mind (or *Nous*), and the Divine Mind, in turn, emanates the World Soul (Psyche). These were called the Three Hypostases, the three underlying states behind the world of the senses. In Neoplatonism, the philosopher (or mystic as they are the same) through spiritual contemplation reverses the path of creation, ascending from Soul to Mind and from Mind back to the One (fig.5).

Here the Imaginal would correspond to the World Soul, the hypostasis immediately above the sense world. Alternatively, the Imaginal realm could be an intermediate region between the World Soul or Psyche and the world of matter and the senses.

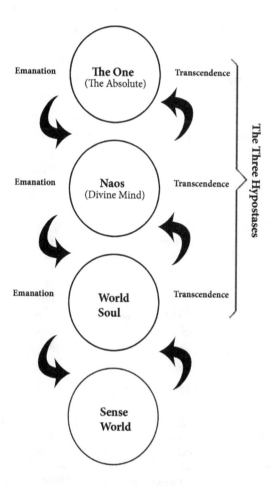

*Fig.5* The philosophy of Plotinus. Every hypostasis (reality) emanates or gives rise to the following reality, without diminishing itself, until the physical universe — the world of the senses — comes about. The philosopher transcends each of these to return to the ultimate reality.

Plotinus didn't emphasize the material universe, seeing it as basically the equivalent of the Indian Vedantic concept of *Maya*. This theme, common to mystics the world over, is that the material universe and physical existence are either ultimately unreal or at least, as in Platonism, a lesser reality and that the only true reality is the transcendent, Enlightenment, Liberation, or Nirvana.

Plotinus' metaphysics was further developed by his successors Porphyry, Iamblichus, and Proclus, with the latter two, inspired in part by the Chaldaean Oracles and late Hellenistic occult syncretism, subdividing or adding other hypostases.

Platonism and Neoplatonism vastly influenced the Medieval, Renaissance, Elizabethan, and Early Modern worldviews.[39]

But it is in the Islamic world that Neoplatonism had the most influence. This is because some of Plotinus' writings were widely believed to be by Aristotle, including the so-called *Theology of Aristotle* and *Book of Causes*. This was reconciled with Islamic theology through Al-Farabi (10th century) and Avicenna (Ibn Sina, 11th century

---

[39] This has been described by the American intellectual historian Arthur Lovejoy in his lecture series, *The Great Chain of Being*. He provides a historical review of the Great Chain of Being in Western exoteric understanding, from Plato to the 18th century. This work, however, simply considers the historical-cultural aspects, and does not pertain to the esoteric and gnostic insights. The latter is described in the late 19th century occult revival, culminating on the one hand in the Theosophy of Blavatsky and her successors (including the New Age movement), and on the other in the syncretic Hermetic Kabbalah of the Golden Dawn of S. L. "McGregor" Mathers and Wynn Westcott, which became the basis for most subsequent Western occultism, via Crowley, Dion Fortune, and others.

Persia). As a result, medieval Islamic metaphysics was based on the four realities of God, the Intellect, the Soul, and the Physical universe, described in immense detail. This Islamic Neoplatonism was also taken up by Sufi mysticism, helping to define its metaphysics.

Here Corbin references Suhrawardi (12th century Persian mystic and founder of Ishraqism or Illuminationism), ibn Arabi (12/13th century Andalusian Sufi), and Ismailism (which includes a form of esotericist Shi'ism) to define the Imaginal (variously referred to as Mithal (similitudes), Malakut (kingdom), Barzakh, Jabulqa and Jabulsa (interworld), and so on.[40]

The Imaginal World is the universe that sits "above" or stands "behind" the Material universe, and there would be other universes or, to use the technical term, *hypostases*, beyond the Imaginal (of course, the Imaginal can itself be divided into many planes of existence), and beyond this are even higher worlds again. These can be referred to as Angelic, Archangelic, or Noetic (of the nature Consciousness or Divine Mind, I have used "Noetic" as a generic description for the hypostasis or hypostases above and prior to the Imaginal but not yet synonymous to the Supreme Source), which are worlds of pure consciousness and divine archetypes. All of these are "sacred" and "divine," in contrast to the familiar mundane world.

As mentioned, Patrick Harpur associates the World Soul with the Jungian Unconscious and Fortean Phenomena.

---

[40] See, for example, *Creative Imagination in the Sufism of Ibn 'Arabi*, Princeton University Press, 1969; *Spiritual Body and Celestial Earth: From Mazdean Iran to Shi'ite Iran*, Princeton University Press, 1977; *The Man of Light in Iranian Sufism*, Shambhala Publications, 1978; and *Swedenborg and Esoteric Islam*, Swedenborg Foundation, 1995.

However, he does not explore the metaphysical and cosmological dimensions the way that Plotinus, Blavatsky, and Corbin do.

From this perspective, the profane-mundane polarity (or subjective and objective) shown in fig.2 pertains only to the lowest sphere of existence and is transcended with the Imaginal and above. "Lowest" is not intended here in any sort of moral value sense; I am not advocating a Coptic Gnostic or Manichaean division of reality into "evil" Matter and "good" Spirit. All dimensions of existence are valid, although evolution in but the material level is *evolving* to perfection, whereas the higher levels of being are eternally perfect (yet also static).

As well as this vertical spectrum from matter to spirit and gross to subtle body,[41] there is also a horizontal polarity, which ties in with the already mentioned polarity of Imagination and Rationalism (section 2). Chinese cosmology and subtle physiology refer to the polarity of *yin* (receptive) and *yang* (creative), which finds parallels with the Indian Tantric *ida* (lunar) and *pingala* (solar) *nadi*s,[42] and even the different types of consciousness associated with the right and left brain hemispheres (spatial/artistic and linear/logical), as first described by American neuroscientist Roger Sperry.[43] Essentially, what

---

[41] For a comprehensive philosophical review on the subtle body, see J. J. Poortman, *Vehicles of Consciousness; The Concept of Hylic Pluralism (Ochema)*, vol I-IV, The Theosophical Society in the Netherlands, 1978. See also Cox, *A Genealogy of the Subtle Body*, for a Western historical and comparative Eastern coverage.

[42] Eliade, Mircea, *Yoga: Immortality and Freedom*; transl. by W. R. Trask, Princeton University Press, 2nd ed. 1969, pp.239-41.

[43] Gazzaniga, Michael (1967), "The Split Brain in Man," *Scientific American*, 217 (2): 24–29.

is being discussed here is the polarity of the individual physico-psycho-spiritual organism, which finds its macrocosmic equivalent in the distinction of the physical and Imaginal universe.

## 9. THE ESOTERIC VERSUS THE JUNGIAN ARCHETYPE

A distinction should be made here between the metaphysical archetypes or hierarchies of celestial intelligences as described, for example, by Corbin on the basis of Ishraqi, Sufi, and Ismaili esotericism and mysticism — and directly equivalent concepts in Late Neoplatonism, Sethian, and Valentinian Gnosticism, and Zoharic, Cordoveran, and Lurianic Kabbalah — and the psychological archetypes of Jungian psychology and individuation. The former can be equated with the Noetic hypostasis (Nous or Mind in fig. 5). They are totally transcendent realities, pertaining to the mystical dimension and representative of higher spiritual insights or "cosmological gnosis."[44] The latter, the Jungian, are symbols of transformation within the psyche and pertain to the Imaginal or intermediate reality beneath the Noetic but above the Physical.

Jung himself, coming from a secular, materialistic perspective, tended to psychologize premodern esotericism and gnosis, reducing it to projections of

---

[44] Arthur Versluis, What is Esoteric? Methods in the Study of Western Esotericism. vol. IV, *Esoterica* <http://esoteric.msu.edu/VolumeIV/Methods.htm> (Retrieved 30 May 2021).

the collective unconscious.[45] In contrast, Corbin, being grounded in Islamic and Iranian esotericism, emphasized the reality of the hypostases while subscribing to a sort of premodern literalism that is just as one-sided as Jung's modernity. Both are describing the same thing, each with great insight, but each at the same time from a partial perspective, like the way a photon can appear either as a particle or a wave, depending on the way it is measured (the so-called Two Slit experiment).

---

[45] See for example *Aion: Researches into the Phenomenology of the Self*, vol 9.2 of the Collected Works, and his three volumes on alchemy: *Psychology and Alchemy*, *Alchemical Studies*, and *Mysterium Coniunctionis*; volumes 12 to 14 of his Collected Works. While Jung's writings are incredibly profound from a phenomenological point of view (as regards the phenomena of consciousness, and the workings of the unconscious psyche) they are also limited from a metaphysical point of view.

## 10. MYTH – A NEW DEFINITION

**M**y basic thesis, then, can be summed up as follows: *Myth is the anthropocentric and anthropomorphic representation of the Imaginal reality and its psychoid archetypes in terms of material-physical, historical, and Egoic-personal narrative.*

Since this is quite a lot of jargon, each of these technical terms should be described in more detail.

*Anthropocentric* means looking at Transpersonal, Imaginal, and transcendent realities from our particular human historical and psychological *perspective*. Obviously, given the incomprehensible vastness of the gross physical cosmos revealed by scientific instruments, let alone of all the other dimensions of existence, we are nothing more than an infinitesimal speck of dust in relation to the big picture. Hence there is a certain Egoic narcissism in even presuming to center this infinity around us. Or if we do center it around ourselves, we must also center it around every other being and thing in the universe, in the sense of the Buddhist metaphor of Indra's Net (*Avatamsaka Sutra*), by which every jewel in Indra's infinite net is shown to contain infinite worlds and Buddhas (also William Blake – "to see infinity in a grain of sand..."). Thus both history (outer reality) and myth (inner reality) make the infinite

55

universe more manageable by portraying it from our limited perspectives.

*Anthropomorphic* means giving human physical, psychological (including mundane-personality, Egoic fantasy, and self-projection), and historical, socio-cultural *characteristics* to nonhuman realities. These are portrayed in terms of mundane physical reality known to everyday waking consciousness, the socio-cultural environment most familiar to both the author and his or her readers (even if it is projected into a fantastical setting), and the psychological dynamics of Ego, Shadow, *Anima/ Animus*, and other personality aspects which make up the limited self and its projections and fantasies. Together, all of these constitute the filters by which the surface consciousness distorts the experiences it receives and the realities it interacts with. So, for example, "*devas*" (spirit beings associated with nature[46]) might be given human characteristics and be represented as a race of physical, biological, (yet also still magical) beings such as elves.

*Imaginal* has already been explained, but to reiterate, it refers to a universal reality that is both (a) the opposite/ complementary polarity to the historical, material-physical, mundane reality (in the sense of *yin* and *yang*, night and day) and (b) intermediate between that physical world and the spiritual-archetypal-divine Noetic reality (in the sense of gross and subtle planes of existence).

---

[46] "*Devas*" in this context derives from Adyar Theosophy and the New Age movement and shouldn't be confused with the original Hindu definition of gods, or for that matter the Buddhist concept of six realms of rebirth, with the *devas*/gods being the most pleasurable. See, for example, Geoffrey Hodson's *Kingdom of the Gods*, Quest Books (the title being a nod to Hindu mythology but that's about all), *The Findhorn Garden: Pioneering a New Vision of Man and Nature in Cooperation*, by The Findhorn Community, and any number of other works.

Along with the transcendent spiritual dimensions, which few can access, the Imaginal is also what gives meaning and purpose to our lives. Without the Imaginal, all existence would appear to surface consciousness as totally pointless. The Collective Unconscious of Jung is a modern psychological description of this same reality, the difference being that I do not derive the Imaginal from any sort of racial or biological memory or other reductionist explanations.

Myth then, by which is meant everything from traditional creation stories to the epics of Homer or Vyasa to contemporary genres in fiction writing, cinema, and more recently even computer gaming, are socio-cultural, anthropomorphic, and materialistic representations of an actual cosmological reality. Just as science and technology enable us to understand, interact with and manipulate the external material-physical world, myths fill the same function regarding the Imaginal, which is the inner world of meaning and purpose, and just as essential as the outer world.

While the archetypes of the Imaginal World are timeless (which is not to deny they follow their own "sacred history"[47]), the external, historical, material-physical world and socio-cultural structures are constantly changing, and knowledge is always advancing.

---

[47] The insight or gnostic glimpse of an Imaginal history (historiosophy, counter-history or meta-history), in which the spiritual world has its own epochs, which are totally different to those of the exterior world, was a theme shared by the esotericist scholars Mircea Eliade, Gershom Scholem, and Henry Corbin, but developed to the greatest degree by the latter. Corbin used terms like history *sui generis*, Imaginal history, or hierohistory (sacred history). See Steven M. Wasserstrom, 1999, *Religion After Religion*, p.159.

This creates a disjunction between the two realities, the Imaginal and the Historical, or Imagination and Reason. Social change and the advance of modernity mean that old myths become either absurd (like a literal belief in the anthropomorphic gods of the Greek pantheon) or frozen into stifling religious literalism with no grounding in modern science (like the creation stories of the Abrahamic religions, which have to be interpreted metaphorically rather than literally).

Because of this disjunction, myths, and hence our representation of the sacred, have to be constantly reinvented and re-envisaged in each historical period, and new myths built from older ones, or even created from scratch. This is the task of the *mythopoeticist*,[48] the myth-maker. Because things constantly change, and yet human beings always require mythic narratives, there will always (or at least as long as humanity remains) be the need for mythopoeticists to readjust the Imaginal narratives in a way that is applicable to the historical and socio-cultural forms of the day.

---

[48] Both mythopoet and mythopoeticist are appropriate words for one who creates myths. The former is probably more etymologically correct. I prefer the latter however, because of the association of "poet" with poetry, and hence of mythopoet as a writer of mythic poetry or of a poet who explores myths, rather than specifically a creator of myths as such in any medium (verse, short story, novel, art, music, cinema, graphic novel, computer game, etc.

## 11. CONSCIOUSNESS, SOCIETY, AND MYTH-MAKING

Anatomically modern humans (*Homo sapiens sapiens*) are known from fossil remains in Ethiopia, about 150 to 200 thousand years old. We can assume there has been little or no evolution or change in the human brain and innate cognitive abilities since that time.

In contrast, cultures, societies, knowledge, and technology have changed markedly. Here I'll adopt Wikipedia's coverage and define culture as "an integrated pattern of human knowledge, belief, and behavior that depends upon the capacity for symbolic thought and social learning" and society as "a social network of people, with relations based on their social status and roles." Following Swiss cultural phenomenologist Jean Gebser, four radically distinct stages of cultural development (Gebser uses the term "mutations of consciousness") can be referred to: Magic, Mythical, Mental-Perspectival, and Integral-Aperspectival. He also refers to an earlier, purely hypothetical, "archaic" stage, but this is not described and can, I believe, be safely discarded. Others have developed similar schemas, the whole constituting a sort of "integral theory of consciousness." Gebser is using myth and mythical in a rather different sense to that of the present essay. By Mythical, he means a particular structure or stage of consciousness and society dominated by myth-based symbolism and understanding. In contrast, I mean specific attributes of the Imagination polarity of consciousness in all stages or structures, deriving from its association with the Imaginal World.

The so-called "Axial period," in which the great world religions and philosophies were developed,[49] includes Mythical and Mental. These cultural stages result from different socio-technological stages. For example, the Magical pertains to the Paleolithic Hunter-Gatherer period of society, the Mythical to settled agriculture and everything from Neolithic to Bronze and Iron-working, while the Mental-Perspectival is the period from the age of Reason to the Industrial Age. Late 20th century technology has resulted in the Information Age, which does not seem to have an equivalent in Gebser's system.

Therefore, myths are not static representations of changeless Platonic truths, but dynamic anthropomorphic socio-cultural representations of those aspects of the Imaginal World that impact human life and society.

---

[49] The term Axial Age (*achsenzeit*, "axistime") was coined by German philosopher Karl Jaspers to describe the period from 800 to 200 B.C.E, during which, similar revolutionary thinking appeared in China, India, and the Occident. (Jaspers, *Vom Ursprung und Ziel der Geschichte* (*The Origin and Goal of History*), via Wikipedia, "Axial Age".) One could extend this period to include the development of Neoplatonism, Advaita Vedanta, other great philosophies, and the rise of Islam. Also, it occurred at different times and different ways in different cultures, civilizations, and spiritual traditions. The Axial Age led to a long religious period which was only overturned with the secular enlightenment, the rise of modernity and the middle class in the West, and, more recently, westernization and industrialization of non-western civilizations like Japan, China, and India. Today the Islamic world remains the only civilization which retains an Axial Age culture, society, and moral code, but even that is only a shadow of its former medieval glory.

And just as culture, society, and worldviews evolve, so do myth and myth-making. When they were composed, the creation stories of animistic, henotheistic, and monotheistic religions (Magic, Mythical, and Axial stages) were legitimate explanations. But as knowledge has advanced (Mental-Perspectival/Modern period), their "scientific" value evaporated. Unless one resorts to fundamentalism, they can only be justified either as fables or as symbolic accounts using archaic belief systems. This is why Imaginal truths have to be recreated with each new age and advancement in human understanding. The mythopoeticist, therefore, is someone who will always have things to do.

My position differs from Gebser's. I discard the redundant Archaic stage, and replace his Integral (a word that is quite meaningless as a blanket term for the next stage of consciousness because of different and contradictory definitions given, for example, by Sri Aurobindo, Gebser, and Ken Wilber) with several future stages, which are the modern mental-perspectival mythopoesis that is projected into the future and in some cases transcends the mental-perspectival all together, becoming not so much Imaginal as eschatological and transcendent, such as Western Transhumanism[50] (nanotech, A.I., human augmentation, genetically augmented posthumans, technological singularity,[51] and so on),

---

[50] For an early introduction and overview, see Damien Broderick, *The Spike – Accelerating into the Unimaginable Future,* Reed Books, 1997 (revised and updated edition published in 2001 as *The Spike: How Our Lives Are Being Transformed by Rapidly Advancing Technologies,* New York: Tom Doherty Associates, 2001). Transhumanist themes are a popular element of the hard science fiction subgenre, especially when depicting a high tech near future; for example the Cyberpunk genre.

[51] Mathematician, computer scientist, and science fiction author

Russian Cosmism's Transhumanist synthesis of science and Orthodox Christianity,[52] Teilhard's Omega Point,[53] and Sri Aurobindo and Mirra Alfassa ("the Mother" of Auroville)'s Supramentalisation (Divinization of Matter).[54] These futuristic, evolutionary, and modernity-informed, and trans-modernity eschatologies have very different mythopoeses to the premodern, mythic stage supernaturalist eschatologies of Persian and Abrahamic religions (Day of Judgment, Resurrection, and so on) and are here referred to as "Transtypal," in contrast to "Archetypal."

Hence each mode (Gebser: "mutation") of consciousness, and each Imaginal time orientation has its own unique mythopoesis.

One could even contrast the backward-looking, "racial memory" archetypes of the collective unconscious with

Vernor Vinge argues in his 1993 essay *The Coming Technological Singularity,* that self-evolving artificial intelligence will soon surpass humanity, ushering in an incomprehensible future. Vinge's ideas were taken up by American inventor and futurist Ray Kurzweil in a series of optimistic books including *The Age of Intelligent Machines* (1990), *The Age of Spiritual Machines* (1999), and *The Singularity Is Near* (2005). See also Acceleration Watch <https://www.accelerationwatch.com/>. For a fictional account, see Charles Stross Accelerando, Orbit/Ace, 2005.

[52] A synthesis of progressive technological futurism and Russian Orthodox Christianity, including both a religious and a purely secular form. See George M. Young, *Russian Cosmists: Esoteric Futurism of Nikolai Fedorov and His Followers*, Oxford University Press, Oxford and New York, 2012.

[53] Pierre Teilhard de Chardin, *The Phenomenon of Man*, Harper and Row, New York, 1959.

[54] Satprem, *Mind of the Cells: Or Willed Mutation of Our Species.* Luc Venet (Translator). Institute for Evolutionary Research, 1982.

what one might call a transtype, like archetypes but projected forward into the future. Or, to be more precise, projecting back from a yet to physically realized Imaginal and physical future; the innovative, creative power of the future. Interestingly, there is a lot of support for the hypothesis called "Retrocausality" in Quantum Physics, which suggests reverse causality, moving backward in time, as a way of explaining quantum events.[55]

---

[55] Lisa Zyga Physicists provide support for retrocausal quantum theory, in which the future influences the past, Phys org, 5 July, 2017, <https://phys.org/news/2017-07-physicists-retrocausal-quantum-theory-future.html>. For a more detailed coverage, Simon Friederich and Peter W. Evans, *Retrocausality in Quantum Mechanics, Stanford Encyclopedia of Philosophy*, 3rd June, 2019. <https://plato.stanford.edu/entries/qm-retrocausality/>.

## 12. A SHORT POTTED HISTORY OF MYTH-MAKING

Up until only several thousand years ago, myth-makers remained anonymous and unknown. At the same time, their creative genius became incorporated into and served as the foundation of the culture as a whole. For tens or even hundreds of thousands of years, mythopoesis took the form of tribal lore and creation stories during the Hunter-Gather stage, where understanding was based on the magical (*sensu* Gebser) paradigm.

With the rise of settled communities, agriculture, the first cities, and civilization (the Mythical stage), it took the form of sacred myths and folktales (see, for example, Joseph Campbell's *Masks of God* series). During this time, the first heroic epic narratives appeared, such as the Sumerian *Epic of Gilgamesh* (1300-1000 B.C.E.).

With the emergence of world religions and philosophies during the Axial Age, these myths and creation stories were often appropriated by institutionalized religion. And the Axial religions themselves are all works of mythopoesis (in the sense that they are sacred and hence symbolic narratives rather than mundane historically documented reports; there was no CNN reporter following Moses or Buddha or Jesus around and recording everything they said and did!). This was also the period from which the first historical names of mythopoets have come down to us, although they are still themselves shrouded in myth and legend. This is myth not as creation narratives or religious dogma but as epic adventures. These were still interpreted historically (literally), despite their supernatural elements. Mention can be made of Homer's *Iliad* and *Odyssey* (8th-9th century B.C.E.), Virgil's *Aeneid* (29-19 B.C.E.), Vyasa's *Mahabharata*, (4th century B.C.E.), the *Ramayana* (400 B.C.E. to 200 C.E.), and the Anglo-Saxon epic of *Beowulf* (c. 750-1000). Although these and other traditional myths may have served an esoteric, initiatory role,[56] they also feature epic heroes, great battles, and supernatural beings, and in this context are no different to contemporary works of myth-making, such as the fantasy writings of J. R. R. Tolkien, the superhero comic stories of Stan Lee, or the space opera of George Lucas.

During the medieval and early modern period, some myths still had strong religious and cosmological — for example, Dante's *Divine Comedy* (early 14th Century) and Milton's *Paradise Lost* (17th Century) — or historical or pseudo-historical — such as Geoffrey of Monmouth's 12th-century history of King Arthur — associations and were respected as such. Other mythopoetic stories, such as the collection of Middle Eastern and Asian folk tales called the *One Thousand and One Nights* (mid-8th to mid-13th century), Chaucer's *Canterbury Tales* (late 14th century), Wu Cheng'en's *Monkey's Journey to the West* (16th Century), the works of Shakespeare (late 16th to early 17th century), and Cervantes' *Don Quixote* (early 17th century) were recognized as just that, stories,

---

[56] Martin Lings, *Symbol and Archetype: A Study of the Meaning of Existence*, (1991, 2006), Fons Vitae Quinta Essentia.

and thus pertaining to the mundane world, rather than the numinous and Imaginal, although this is no way diminished their ability to thrill or amuse.

*Fig.6.* Adam and Eve Driven Out of Paradise. From John Milton, *Paradise Lost,* Illustration by John Martin (Book 12, line 641), Chatfield & Co. 1827.

The 1667/1674 original is one of the great mythopoetic epics of the English language. Like all such accounts, it is nostalgic and backward-looking, deeply embedded in the religious mythology and theology of the time.

## 13. THE ORIGIN OF THE NOVEL

**F**urther radical development in myth-making took place with the rise of secular modernity. As a result of the 17th century age of reason and the 18th-century secular enlightenment, rationalism (reason, empiricism, historicism, scientific method) to a large extent replaced myth (traditional religion) as the source of authority regarding Big Questions. Putting things simplistically, this was the transition from what Gebser (*The Ever Present Origin*) called the Mythical to the Mental-Perspectival stage, or from what postmodernists and, following them, Wilber (*Sex, Ecology, Spirituality*), refer to as the Premodern and the Modern.

Rudolf Steiner said the same thing regarding the rise of Individuality, which although a necessary stage in human and cosmic evolution, is also associated with materialism and Ahriman.[57] Such a transition had already occurred in the age of classical Greece and Rome, beginning with the rise of the natural sciences and the Greek theatrical culture of the 6th to 3rd centuries B.C.E., but following the rise of institutionalized Christianity and the fall of

---

[57] Rudolf Steiner, *The Influences of Lucifer and Ahriman*, Anthroposophic Press, 1993.

Rome, this nascent modernity was swallowed up by axial-mythic monotheistic religion.

However, what was different with modernity was that widespread literacy and affordable literature via the print media meant that information was more widely available and readily disseminated than in the classical period. In the Axial Age, the growth of rational and secular culture and society (in classical Athens and Rome, for example) was unsustainable due to too few resources and primitive technology (hand-copied manuscripts rather than printing). Hence philosophy and proto-science were lost when Hellenistic and Roman civilizations fell to Christian monotheism. Whereas the rise of modernity was tied in with a technological civilization that was on the ascendant and has, only now in the first decades of the 21st century, reached the tipping point regarding resources and the limits to growth (peak oil, environmental collapse, overpopulation, etc.).

But the 17th and 18th-century transition from the Mythic to the Rational does not mean that mythopoesis is dead. Instead, mythopoesis became less associated with religion and more with *individual* (note Steiner) story-telling. The rise of the individual story-teller, as opposed to the cultural mythopoeticist or religious prophet, can be traced through the emergence of the heroic and satirical romances and "*belles lettres*" of the 16th and following centuries, the novels (literally "new"), romances, pseudo-histories, and satires of the late 17th and early 18th centuries. Leisure reading and popular (as opposed to classic) literature began much earlier, with the chapbooks of the 16th to early 19th century, frequently denounced by Religious leaders for their titillating content. The novel, as we know it, emerges with the origin of the middle class with increased literacy and leisure time at the beginning of the 18th century. Readers, primarily women, read novels for entertainment that was also social education,[58] hence the rise of the Romance novel featuring realistic as opposed to mythic protagonists. During the American Civil War, Dime Novels about detectives and Indian raids were popular with soldiers. The expansion of the railroad saw railroad literature, the forerunner of the airport novel. Then there was the American paperback boom of the forties and fifties. Even now, the association between leisure and lowbrow literature persists, even if it is propagated more by the publishing industry.[59]

Big publishing houses have to make money and, like movie studios, will only print what they know will sell. Hence it is very easy for an established author to sell a sequel, no matter how poorly written, but very difficult for a new author, no matter how talented, to get their work accepted. This reinforces a monotony and lack of diversity in print, just as there is the same uniformity in cinema and video games, as well as the cross-over between genres so that there is a single meta-media whose only purpose is to make money. Fortunately, this is changing, with the transition away from the mass-produced novel of the

---

[58] Denis Donogue, Alternative history of the novel vogue, *Weekend Australian Review*, June 12-13, 2010, p.22, a review of Steven Moore, *The Novel: An Alternative History*. Moore apparently uses the word novel to refer to any work of fictional or mythic narrative. I prefer the more traditional definition, which is tied in with the emergence not just of individualization in the story teller, but also the middle class, and hence modernity as we know it, in the socio-cultural milieu. The Wikipedia page on the Novel also includes a detailed historical review of the development of the early novel and its predecessors.

[59] Meredith Blake, Rethinking the Beach Read, *The New Yorker* – The Book Bench, June 11, 2010 <http://www.newyorker.com/online/blogs/books/2010/06/rethinking-the-beach-read.html>.

20th century to electronic publishing in the early 21st. This empowers both authors (who can now easily get their work in print) and readers, who now have a more comprehensive range of material to choose from.[60] The extent to which the rise of e-publishing impacts on the print industry remains to be seen.

The popularity of the novel, the relative ease with which it can be produced, and the cultural transformations wrought by modernity and social individualization freed up mythopoesis, so it was no longer the sole province of either institutionalized religious ecclesia or grassroots folk culture, but could become the occupation of anyone with the imagination and energy to articulate their own stories and myths in written form. Meanwhile, cinema, television, and now computer games provide immersive visual worlds that have taken the place of traditional religious mythopoesis and reinvented traditional archetypes in new and contemporary forms.

*Fig.7.* Rochester and Jane Eyre. From a watercolor drawing by Frederick Walker, A.R.A., 1899. *Jane Eyre* by Charlotte Bronte is a coming-of-age story that focuses on the moral and spiritual development of its eponymous heroine. The earliest example of a first-person perspective novel, Charlotte Bronte's revolutionary style of writing, where events are colored by the stream of consciousness of the narrator, marks an advance not only on premodern mythological classics like the *Divine Comedy* and *Paradise Lost* but also on the novels of that came before. Combining social criticism, romance, and a subjective perspective, it is representative of the revolution of story-telling away from grand mythic tropes in favor of the biography — or in this case, autobiography — of the fictional protagonist. Originally divided into 38 chapters in three volumes in 1847, a condensed version appeared as a classic black and white movie starring Orson Welles and Joan Fontaine almost a century later, in 1943.

---

[60] Regan McMahon, Authors using Internet to get their books out, SF Gate, Tuesday, May 25, 2010 <http://www.sfgate.com/cgi-bin/article.cgi?f=/c/a/2010/05/24/DDTJ1DIJ95.DTL>.

## 14. OTHER CONTEMPORARY MYTHOPOETIC MEDIAS

**T**raditional epics, such as *Beowulf*, were written in such a way as to evoke the drama of the narrative in their listeners, and, especially in the hands of a skilled reciter, these were very much the Hollywood blockbusters of their time.

Medieval mystery and miracle plays (mostly 10th to the 16th century) used Biblical stories accompanied by choral singing. The morality play was a form of religious theatrical entertainment in Europe during the 15th and 16th centuries. Both were supplanted by the rise of professional theatre, for example, in Tudor England.

Today the media and technology have changed, but not the content. Frank McConnell, a professor of English at the University of California, considers that film is a perfect vehicle for myth-making, as it "strives toward the fulfillment of its projected reality in an ideally associative, personal world."[61] The American Classical Western, for example, represents the Arthurian knight and the principle of chivalry. However, this was replaced in later developments of the genre by the cowboy as a

---

[61] McConnell, Frank. *Storytelling and Mythmaking*, New York, Oxford: Oxford University Press, 1979, cited via "Mythopoeic (genre)" on Wikipedia.

professional outlaw or anti-hero.[62] By generating a far more overwhelming visual and auditory impact, Cinema and its little brother Television[63] have pushed aside the old theatre performances, musicals, comedies, and other stage shows, which have become a subculture of the artistic community. It may be that the age of Mythopoetic cinema is over. With the decline of creativity in Hollywood due to interminable rewriting of screenplays and the need to make returns from increasingly expensive multi-million dollar budgets, the big studios have resorted to empty whizz-bang special effects, old franchises, banal comedies, recycling comic book superheroes, and even computer games for inspiration. There are still a few examples that have managed to buck the trend, such as Peter Jackson's 2001-2003 adaptation of *Lord of the Rings* and James' Cameron's 2009 mythopoetic sci-fi epic *Avatar*, but these seem to be the exception rather than the rule.

The so-called "comic book" represents a media form transitional between the novel (individual narrative and dialogue) and cinema (visual). Comics book superheroes such as Jerry Siegel and Joe Shuster's Superman, Bob Kane and Bill Finger's Batman, and Jack Kirby and Stan

---

[62] Will Wright, *Sixguns and Society: a Structural Study of the Western.* University of California Press, 1975.

[63] The introduction of large widescreen flat panel technology has provided home viewers with an increasingly cinematic experience, further enhanced by "home cinema" packages. Cinema to be competitive has to resort to gimmicks, such as 3D and IMAX screens, which create an even greater sensory overload. I observed this with the sci-fi epic and special effects extravaganza *Avatar* on the IMAX in 3D. It is almost like being immersed in an Imaginal World, albeit an ersatz Imaginal World. Nevertheless, the movie did make a huge impression on me, an association of the incredible visuals of both the CGI and the screen technology, and an empathic and pro-ecological message I strongly resonated with, and even mythopoetic elements.

Lee's Fantastic Four, Spiderman, and X-Men can also be considered the modern equivalent of the gods, heroes, and saints of classical and medieval mythology.[64] Although this is more debatable, it has even been suggested that the inspiration for the modern book superhero can be found in secret societies and 19th-20th century occultism.[65] In Japan, *manga* has been an acceptable literary art form since the late 18th century, and similarly, *anime* does not have the juvenile connotations that "cartoons" have in the West. In contrast to the bumbling Daffy Duck and trickster-like Bugs Bunny, Japanese anime tends to feature poignant child-heroes like Osamu Tezuka's Astro Boy (in Japanese *Tetsuwan Atomu* – "Mighty Atom"). Modern Japanese manga dates back to the American Occupation and post-Occupation years (1945 to early 1960s) when a great burst of artistic creativity accompanied a political and economic reconstruction. But in the West, it was only in the late 1980s that the comic book gave way to the graphic novel, acquiring a more adult reputation with Frank Miller's reinvention of Batman as the tortured, almost anti-hero, Dark Knight. In recent years, in keeping with this change to more "adult" entertainment, best-selling prose authors have been migrating to the comics/graphic novel format, collaborating with artists either in original works or adopting prose text.[66]

---

[64] Thomas Roberts, The Mythos of the Superheroes and the Mythos of the Saints, Mythcon 32, abstracts, p.16 <http://www.electroephemera.com/images/mc32pb.pdf> (Retrieved 25 May 2010). I do not agree with the premise that this "is the only case in human history in which a people has invented a mythos it knew to be story-telling"; the above examples show that is not the case.

[65] Chris Knowles, *Our Gods Wear Spandex: The Secret History of Comic Book Heroes,* Weiser Books (2007).

[66] BEA 2010: Bestselling Prose Authors Turn to Graphic Novels by Ada Price Jun 01, 2010 <http://publishersweekly.com/pw/by-topic/book-

Media like books, cinema, television, and comics/graphic novels do not allow any reader/viewer impact. The reader or viewer is carried along passively, and this is much more overwhelming in television and cinema than in books and comics, where the imagination is allowed input.

Hence the role-playing game, beginning with Gary Gygax and Dave Arneson's *Dungeons & Dragons* — itself heavily inspired by Tolkien's Middle Earth mythos — in 1974, represented an important breakthrough in allowing individual participation in the unfolding narrative, even if it was limited to a very small subculture, with the actual story involving little more than fighting monsters and finding treasure. As the name reveals, the role-playing game consists of the player or participant taking on a particular role or character and having adventures with friends who play other characters in the team. Outcomes of battles are determined by player strengths and the role of dice. The game is conducted and referred to by another person, the Dungeon Master (or Game Master). While *Dungeons & Dragons* remains the most popular role-playing game, it was soon joined by other genres, such as space opera (inspired by science fiction literature and movies like *Star Wars*), horror (vampires and werewolves feature prominently), and other fantasy adventures.

Interactive computer games are a more recent innovation. These are somewhat like a role playing game but with the player controlling his or her character or "avatar" in the game. Because everything is done by computer, there is no need for rules, dice, or even other players. Monotonously, the most popular genres were (beginning in 1992 with *Wolfenstein 3D*, and followed a year later by

news/comics/article/43371-bea-2010-bestselling-prose-authors-turn-to-graphic-novels.html>.

*Doom*) and still are the "first-person shooter," in which the player has to face and mow down hordes of enemies and/ or monsters. In the mid to late noughties, as computer technology and production values have increased, games have become increasingly cinematic, and also – because of increasing financial investment, increasingly limited and formulaic. Fast internet bandwidth and banks of dedicated computers have made possible shared universes (Massively Multiplayer Online Role-Playing Games) that thousands can participate in and have even spawned virtual communities and social networking. Some of these, such as *EverQuest* and *World of Warcraft*, employ classic Tolkienesque fantasy tropes. Others, such as *Eve Online*, are based on science fiction space opera. Especially recently, advances in computing power have allowed computer games to include vast interactive open worlds, such as in Rockstar's 2010 release *Red Dead Redemption* (by Rockstar Games, which with Blizzard Entertainment's *World of Warcraft* was one of the two games that defined the industry in terms of power and popularity,[67] such centralization seems to be becoming increasingly common in the media and entertainment industry, as demand for special effects drives production cost ever higher) which has almost single-handedly reinvented the Cowboy epic. Unfortunately, the bulk of computer games have still been unable to break free of the one-dimensional violence endemic to the genre. Whether this is due to the technical difficulties of creating and playing a fully interactive universe with multiple life choices, game paths, and more realistic player characters, or simply a lack of imagination on the part of game

---

[67] Seth Schiesel, Awaiting Holidays' Electronics (and Sales), *The NY Times* Television/Video Games, June 11, 2010 <http://www.nytimes.com/2010/06/12/arts/television/12games.html>.

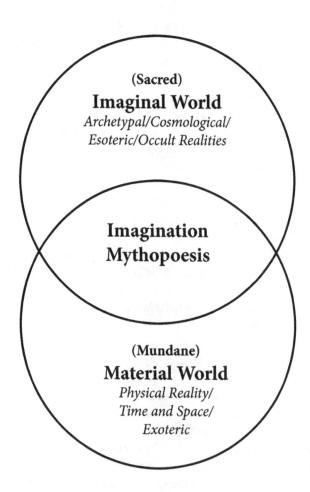

*Fig.8.* Imagination and Myth as mediators between the Imaginal and the Mundane world, possessing the characteristics of both.

designers is still debatable.[68] A Hollywood media industry long bereft of ideas has been using computer games as the basis for bland sci-fi/fantasy/horror movies for years. And while the literary migration to video games can be seen especially with the adaptation of novels by best-selling thriller writers like Tom Clancy (*Rainbow Six*, *Splinter Cell*, etc.), now the influence is starting to go the other way, with shooter games becoming the inspiration for novels in which protagonists become, in one reviewer's evocative phrase, little more than "pixelated agents of violence."[69]

---

[68] A Bit of the Old UltraViolence, *Games TM*, no. 94, Imagine Publishing, pp.88-93

[69] Geordie Williamson "Video killed the literary star," *Weekend Australian Review*, June 12-13, 2010, pp.20-21; a review of John Birmingham's *After America*. Birmingham began as one of the most talented new lights in Australian contemporary fiction, with *He Died with a Falafel in his Hand* (1994), a hilarious account of his sharehousing experiences. Since then he has followed fellow Australian and best-selling author Matthew Reilly into the American war/thriller genre. Having read the first volume of his alternative World War II time travel saga (*World War 2.1: Weapons of Choice*, 2004, essentially a revisioning of director Don Taylor's disappointing 1980 movie *The Final Countdown*, about a modern aircraft carrier that travels back in time to just prior the 1941 attack on Pearl Harbor), it seemed a shame that the delicious black humor of his earlier work on sharehousing was not retained.

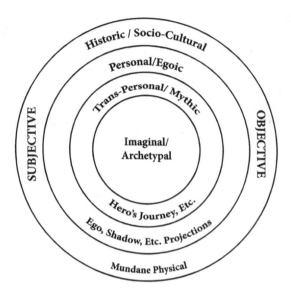

*Fig.9.* The spectrum of consciousness, the different levels of which together make up mythopoesis. These can be referred to as (from material to spiritual) the Historic/Mundane, Egoic/Personal, Mythic/ Transpersonal, Imaginal/Archetypal, and Transcendent (not shown because it transcends all the other levels). For the sake of simplicity, this diagram replaces the triangular model of fig.2 with a more linear "Great Chain of Being" sequence, as shown in fig.4. The subjective-objective polarity is the same as in figures 1 and 3. In keeping with the "inward" model (e.g., the five koshas of Advaita Vedanta, which veil the true Self), the most "spiritual" level is shown at the center, although the diagram could be reversed to show the material level in the center. The Historic and Socio-Cutural is the external physical and cultural reality, the Personal Egoic is the personal (both Profane-Egoic and Mundane-Personal – see fig.11) psyche with its projections, ideals and interactions with the inner (Transpersonal and Mythic) and outer (socio-cultural, historical, and physical) world. The mythic and transpersonal is the individual and collective experience of the Imaginal/Archetypal dimension. Beyond even this, the Transcendent and the Noetic are the purely spiritual realities.

## 15. MYTH AND GLOBAL SYNCRETISM

**T**echnology is not the only way modern story-telling and myth-making differs from that of previous centuries. There is also the increasingly global, multicultural, yet blandly consumerist nature of today's society.

Our ancestors almost certainly spent most of their lives limited to a single culture, religion, and locality. The rest of the world was known dimly, if at all, and only then through the distorting filter (and often Shadow-projection) of their local society and religion. With the printed book, international commerce, world politics, the mass media, and the Internet, there has been the progressive development of the noosphere or Global Brain. And as the world becomes more interconnected, syncretism will inevitably arise in myth-making by juxtaposing different cultures, themes, and tropes. For example, two or more diverse, even unrelated, elements may appear in a single story, the so-called "mash" or "mash-up."[70] The overall effect is a sort of surrealism, just

---

[70] See Television Tropes & Idioms Monster Mash <http://tvtropes.org/ pmwiki/pmwiki.php/Main/MonsterMash>. The classic example of the "Monster Mash" was the now forgotten 1987 movie *The Monster Squad*, featuring Dracula, the Wolf Man, The Mummy, Frankenstein's Monster, and the Fish Man. A more modern version of this is the

as dreams are often mashups or jumbles of conscious experiences that have sunk into the subconscious. Mythopoetic mashups thus combine two or more mythoi in a surreal manner. And the more potent the mythos, the more likely it is to be juxtaposed against another mythos. Take the rich contemporary mythos of the Wild

---

2004 action/horror film *Van Helsing*, a disappointing adaptation of Bran Stoker's famous vampire hunter (the macho man hero is the only one to remain unchanged at the end of the story, representing the static superficiality of the profane Ego, and the total antithesis of the authentic hero's journey). Actually sci fi/fantasy/horror, television, roleplaying, and cinematic universes increasingly have vampires, werewolves, ghosts, and other creatures appearing in the same story. Alan Moore's 1999 graphic novel *The League of Extraordinary Gentlemen* brings together heroic figures from totally unrelated mythoi such as Mina Harker of Bram Stoker's *Dracula*, Captain Nemo of Jules Verne's *20,000 Leagues under the Sea*, Allan Quatermain of H. Rider Haggard *King Solomon's Mines*, Dr. Jekyll of Robert Louis Stevenson's *Dr. Jekyll and Mr Hyde*, H. G. Wells' The Invisible Man, and Dr Cavor (from different stories), Sax Rohmer's Fu Manchu, and Arthur Conan Doyle's Professor Moriarty (arch-enemy of Sherlock Holmes). The popular *Buffy The Vampire Slayer* TV series (1997-2003) is a classic monster mash with vampires, demons, witches, and werewolves. Related to Mash is "Mash Up", which refers to music, video, or digital media, which combines and modifies parts of existing works to create an entirely new work. In music this is an established genre, whereas in video (see especially YouTube), it generally involves combining totally unrelated multiple sources for the purposes of comedy or satire. I use terms like mash and mashup in a creative sense however, to describe any creative work or imagined universe that incorporates or juxtaposes, in either a comical or a serious way, tropes, characters, and settings from unrelated mythoi. Such mashes should be distinguished from philosophical synthesis. Teilhard de Chardin synthesized Christianity and Darwinism; see especially his classic and epic work *The Phenomenon of Man*. This represents a grand cosmological and integrative narrative, of which the only other example of this sort that I know is Sri Aurobindo's *The Life Divine*, and it is hard to find two more disparate "creation stories" than that. But it is not a "mashup", because there is the sense of integration and synthesis, whereas mash-up implies juxtaposition, and hence humor and satire, but sometimes also epic adventure within that context.

West. Fantastical Fiction frequently pits cowboys against elements not found in traditional Wild West mythoi, such as dinosaurs, spaceships, or horror.[71]

---

[71] Ray Harryhausen *The Valley of Gwangi* (1969), an early mash of two totally different genres which pitted cowboys against dinosaurs. In Joss Whedon's *Firefly* television series (2002-3, very poorly served by the Fox Network but still gathered a loyal fanbase) it's cowboys and spaceships. In the 1996 alternate history roleplaying game *Deadlands* written by Shane Lacy Hensley, it's Western, horror, and "Steampunk" genres.

## 16. MYTH, IMAGINATION, AND THE IMAGINAL

**I**magination, especially transpersonal, mythopoetic, imagination, constitutes not only the opposite/complementary psychological pole to rationalism but also serves as the mediator between the socio-cultural and individual psychological (Egoic-personality) dimensions on the one hand and universal Imaginal realities on the other. As Henry Corbin suggests, and I fully agree, Imagination, in the transpersonal, creative and intuitive sense of the word, is not simply subjective fantasizing, or even a distinct but valid mode of creativity (although it is that as well), but the way we experience, process, and interact with the Imaginal world. To reiterate the central thesis of the present essay, Imagination takes Imaginal influences and anthropomorphizes them in personal psychological and collective socio-cultural forms that provide personal and collective meaning.

Although the higher imagination may transcend myth and become a form of gnosis, which allows access to the (and ultimately the Noetic and transcendent) realities directly, this being the goal of esotericism,[72] no conventional

---

[72] See for example Antoine Faivre *Access to Western Esotericism*. Faivre's school of "esoterology" differs from the neo-Sufi Traditionalist

myth-making portrays the Imaginal World as it is. There is always mediation and distortion by the intervening layers of self and society. That is what makes it myth-making, as opposed to immediate revelation. Indeed, direct revelation and gnosis of the Imaginal, Noetic, and Transcendent realities would be incomprehensible to any who are not gnostically informed and have a grounding in one or preferably more spiritual teachings and contemplative techniques. It is only the anthropocentric historical and anthropomorphic Mythic collective unconscious that make even a small aspect of Imaginal, Noetic, and Transcendent revelation understandable and familiar to the common consciousness. Mythopoesis, in other words, takes sacred and revelatory archetypes and translates them into the familiar forms and symbols of everyday life. That is why I refer to myth (and hence mythopoesis) as the anthropomorphic and anthropocentric representation of the Imaginal.

This process involves the juxtaposition of several elements, perhaps as many as four or five, in very profound myths. As shown in fig.5, these elements constitute a spectrum of being from external reality to Imaginal archetypes and beyond. These elements or layers can be described as follows:

- The *historical mundane* level. All story-telling and myth-making has to be grounded in some historical and objective fact. Otherwise, it is meaningless. As physical beings, we require material points of reference. These are then modified and used as building blocks by the

---

(Guenon, Schuon, etc.) "esotericism", although there are also many points of commonality.

creative imagination to represent the more inward elements. Egoic and Mythic story-telling is still primarily based on the author's individual and socio-cultural experiences, influences and conditioning, from external reality. Historical story-telling can also take more external forms such as factual history, historical fiction, social commentary, satire, or autobiography. Even factual history on its own can be mythopoetic, as shown by 18th century English historian Edward Gibbon's six-volume *The History of the Decline and Fall of the Roman Empire*, which set the tone for all subsequent historical methodology.

- The *mundane personality* and *profane Egoic* level: This includes the individual Ego along with personalized archetypes as conscious or unconscious fantasy projections, romantic idealism, and superficial Shadow-projection monsters. Such personalized archetypes constitute diluted versions of transpersonal/ mythic archetypes such as the Shadow (repressed or denied contents), Anima/Animus (romantic idealism), and Wise Old Man or Woman (Mentor). On this level, story-telling may be simplistic and trope – and cliché-driven to the extreme,[73] as in the Western mass-media

---

[73] Numerous examples can be found at List of Science Fiction Clichés — Resources for Science Fiction Writers — <http://www.cthreepo. com/writing/cliche.shtml>. Note that while writers are strenuously advised (and correctly so) to avoid clichés (do an internet search for "clichés to avoid" or similar phrases, or consult any book on "how to write fiction"), the presence of clichés seems to be *de rigueur* for film and television, as the List of Clichés cited above and a brief glance through the Television Tropes & Idioms wiki at tvtropes.org reveals. This is an example of the stultifying and deadening effect of mass media; very often only the most brainless films and TV shows

machine, subtle and more demanding, as in independent film and some "book club" literature, or combinations of the two.

- The transpersonal or *Mythic* level: This represents a sort of transitional level between the sacred or Imaginal and the profane or Egoic, with many mythic narratives paradoxically incorporating both and thus appealing to both the higher and lower aspects of human nature. At this level, the personal and the historical of the preceding two stages are subsumed under, or become symbols for, universal symbols, impersonal archetypes. These symbols and archetypes become gateways to the Imaginal. Such mythic-transpersonal story-telling can be initiatory in nature (as in traditional esotericism) or even just have the effect of expanding or enhancing the consciousness of the reader/viewer/participant. This is mythopoesis proper and most historical, and all contemporary myths belong here.

- The *Imaginal* level: Here, story-telling as we know it is replaced by occult and initiatory accounts and sacred or numinous experiences. Very little of this actually becomes assimilated into the popular consciousness. The Imaginal, unlike the Mythic, requires going beyond Egoic wish-fulfillment and projections altogether.

- The *transcendent*, Noetic, and Divine realities, beyond the Imaginal, which constitute pure Realization ("Spiritual Enlightenment") that

---

are allowed. The reason being that those who hold the purse strings in regard to such things, and are, therefore, concerned at getting a return for their investments, assume that Viewers Are Morons (Television Tropes & Idioms <http://tvtropes.org/pmwiki/pmwiki.php/Main/ViewersAreMorons>.)

equally transcends all levels. The transcendent appears only very rarely and indirectly, in the form of spiritual allegories or in direct accounts of transcendent experience. However, third-person accounts or hagiographies (biographies of saints) more properly belong under the Mythic sphere.

Each of these elements produces a different type of story-telling, as do their various combinations. However, the more mythopoesis excludes the Egoic dimension and is centered around the inner or Mythic gateways to the Imaginal, the more potent it is.

The Imaginal World — the source of creative inspiration — is the opposite of the mundane empirical world and, even more so, of the mundane/profane ego consciousness. The Ego, left to itself, can only create banal wish-fulfillment fantasies, such, let us say, being impossibly competent or attractive (the so-called Mary Sue/Gary Stu), narcissistic sexual scenarios, or getting revenge on someone who has wronged them. Sometimes there'll be more trivial stuff about friends or family and everyday pastimes mixed in. Many blockbuster movies are of this type; all glitzy special effects and no story beyond a string of clichés and crude author avatar wish-fulfillment. The same goes for poor-quality self-published material.

This is because quality writing requires archetypes and symbols of transformation, which exist in the Imaginal world and above; that is, they exist in the opposite realm to the mundane/profane Ego. However, the Ego can access these higher realities by opening itself utilizing gnosis, higher imagination, intuition, and tapping into the "higher unconscious" (to the Imaginal and higher worlds). All great storytelling and mythopoesis come from these regions.

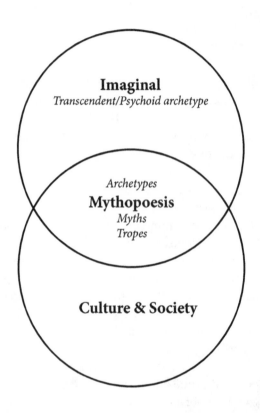

*Fig.10.* Mythopoesis then takes place at the junction of the human world of cultures and societies, and the transcendent Imaginal World, and incorporates archetypes (which are the closest to the pure Imaginal World), myths, and tropes (which pertain to the ordinary world).

In the context of the present essay, the Ego is the source of lower imagination, that lower imagination being what helps feed and maintain it's delusional (but still necessary as regards the evolution of consciousness) opinion of itself as a super-powered separative entity and center of the universe. Hence Egoic fiction, to be considered later, with its vicarious gratification and reinforcing of narcissistic fantasies. By far, the majority of the output of mass media belongs in this category. While providing helpful entertainment for those who are still at the predominantly Egoic level, it is totally stifling for all those who aspire beyond. Whereas reason is concerned with the mundane empirical world of facts and academic study, imagination is concerned with inner narrative and symbolism, whether it be profane or sacred.

Today we live in a society that privileges skeptical rationalism over imagination, science over myth, and mundane over sacred, but the truth is that one is not better than the other. Instead, each serves a different role, and both are equally necessary. But they are also both equally restrictive if one limits oneself to only one to the exclusion of the other (the same applies to any partial approach). Both rationalism and imagination, and both spirituality and modernity, are equally essential for an integral transformation of the entire being and society as a whole.

## 17. ARCHETYPE AND TROPE

Imaginal events and archetypes are distinguished from mundane personality and profane Egoic tropes and projections in that the Imaginal elements are *numinous*. They possess a power or presence of sacredness and divinity,[74] which means they incorporate transcendent and transpersonal dimensions. This is the nature of the Imaginal World, or as Jung would say of the Archetype; it is overwhelming and numinous. And being numinous, such mythic symbols and events are captivating and powerfully transmitted in society from individual to individual and generation to generation. They are, in other words, potent examples of what British evolutionary biologist Richard Dawkins calls "memes"[75] (however, not all memes need be Mythic or Imaginal, many are only ego personality level).

---

[74] Rudolf Otto *The Idea of the Holy*.

[75] Richard Dawkins, *The Selfish Gene*. By analogy with genes of hereditary science, memes are units of cultural ideas, symbols or practices, transmitted from one mind to another through writing, speech, gestures, rituals, or other imitable phenomena. Like genes, memes are considered to replicate and evolve in quasi-Darwinian fashion in response to environmental (in this case socio-cultural) pressures. It should be emphasized that not all scientists accept this interpretation, which from a semiotic perspective can be quite naïve and unsophisticated. Nevertheless, when considering the power of myths, and how certain modern mythoi become so popular, I find it a useful, even if simplistic, approach.

As mentioned, archetypes are universal motifs and symbols that repeatedly reoccur across cultures and history and even spontaneously in dreams, fantasies, and visions.

According to Jung, archetypes never occur culturally or mimetically in their pure form. When they appear as myths, stories, art, religion, and zeitgeists, they are colored by that particular time and culture, expressing the local fads or reflecting social concerns.

These mythic and universal forms become tropes when they are culturally determined and recurring in story making and popular media.

Initially, the word "trope" referred to a turn of phrase or the use of figurative language for artistic effect. More recently, it has come to be used for describing commonly recurring literary and rhetorical devices, motifs, or clichés in creative works. In this context, a trope is a theme or motif within a piece of storytelling that helps further the story or set it within a genre.[76]

Hence we can distinguish between archetype, myth, and trope.

*Archetypes* are psychic attractors or symbols of transformation that pertain to the Imaginal World. In addition to the archetype in itself, the "psychoid archetype," which exists independently of the physical

---

[76] See for example the vast and encyclopedic TV Tropes wiki <http://tvtropes.org/> which includes numerous examples of each trope not only in television but cinema, print, anime, manga, comics/graphic novels, and sometimes even real life.

world and the individual psyche, there is also the archetype as a representation of the collective unconscious that appears in myth, legends, dreams, and so on.

*Myths* represent certain particular themes or archetypes and hence pertain to the representation of the Imaginal World, and the sacred and the human encounter with it.

*Tropes* represent more specific themes, as they appear in storytelling relating to the personal, socio-cultural, and Egoic sphere.

While the number of major archetypes is probably few, the range of possible minor themes and tropes (whether universal, socially and culturally conditioned or both) is practically limitless.

This is why *Lord of the Rings*, *Star Wars*, *Harry Potter*, and the *Matrix* contain similar themes. It also explains why tropes are often interchangeable across genres. So Space Opera, although science fiction, is very similar to high fantasy. Except instead of magic, there is futuristic tech. Instead of an alternate Earth, there is the Galaxy. Instead of magical humanoid races, there are humanoid aliens. However, literary space opera tends to be more creative in employing non-humanoid aliens than movie or TV sci-fi, as writers don't have to worry about human actors, prosthetics, or CGI. They are saying the same thing, differing only in details.

The distinction between universal archetype and cultural trope is not always obvious, with common themes appearing across franchises being equally archetypes and tropes. Tropes can often refer to mythic themes and variations as they appear in the personal, socio-cultural, and Egoic sphere.

As building blocks of myths, folklore, and modern storytelling, the purpose of tropes is to both veil and represent the Imaginal. The Imaginal in its raw, daimonic form is too disorientating, irrational, and even terrifying, to be received by the Ego. Hence it has to be presented in the predigested form of a story via the creativity of the artist or author who translates these Imaginal inspirations into familiar settings, themes, and stock character types.

## 18. STORYTELLING AND TROPES

As mentioned, tropes are the building blocks that the myth or story is composed of. They are recurring themes that may be profound or glib, universal, or pertaining to contemporary fads.[77]

While inwardly, tropes point to and reveal archetypes and so have a universal nature, outwardly or culturally, they may define or describe a genre, character, narrative, or plot twist. There are even aesthetic tropes, such as anime characters having hair of every shade, including blue, green, pink, and so on.[78]

Character Tropes apply across all genres. For example, a character could be an Action Girl, a Swashbuckler, a Mentor, a Child Prodigy, an Annoying Comic Sidekick, and so on. There could be a group of characters, which perhaps is an overlap of Character and Narrative. The Five Man Band is a common trope with any genre or

---

[77] See, for example, these YouTube videos: Terrible Writing Advice <https://www.youtube.com/channel/UC3ogrx6d9oohf6D42G44j1A>, and Overly Sarcastic Productions – Trope Talk <https://www.youtube.com/playlist?list=PLDb22nlVXGgcljcdyDk80bBDXGyeZjZ5e>.

[78] You Gotta Have Blue Hair – TV Tropes <https://tvtropes.org/pmwiki/pmwiki.php/Main/YouGottaHaveBlueHair> (Retrieved 31 May, 2021).

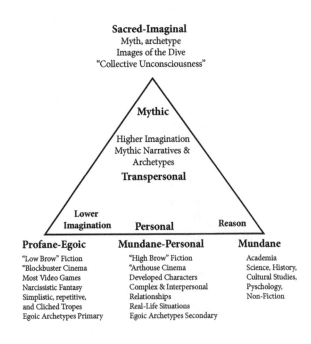

**Sacred-Imaginal**
Myth, archetype
Images of the Dive
"Collective Unconsciousness"

**Mythic**

Higher Imagination
Mythic Narratives &
Archetypes

**Transpersonal**

**Lower Imagination**    **Personal**    **Reason**

| **Profane-Egoic** | **Mundane-Personal** | **Mundane** |
|---|---|---|
| "Low Brow" Fiction | "High Brow" Fiction | Academia |
| "Blockbuster Cinema | "Arthouse Cinema | Science, History, |
| Most Video Games | Developed Characters | Cultural Studies, |
| Narcissistic Fantasy | Complex & Interpersonal | Pyschology, |
| Simplistic, repetitive, | Relationships | Non-Fiction |
| and Cliched Tropes | Real-Life Situations | |
| Egoic Archetypes Primary | Egoic Archetypes Secondary | |

*Fig.11.* Types of literature. This diagram is an elaboration of figures 2 and 9. On the exoteric level of surface consciousness (*bottom of diagram*), there is a spectrum from factual and objective non-fiction (*lower right*), through various grades of realistic or less realistic fiction, to the completely fictional and subjective egoic fantasies (*lower left*). The further towards the egoic, the cheaper and tackier the narrative, yet also the more accessible and appealing, because the lower emotional being seeks such gratification. There is also a "vertical" (on this diagram, but more properly "inward" spectrum or gradation from personal (profane-mundane) to mythic and transpersonal, which is the realm of mythopoesis. This is itself transitional (fig.9) between the exoteric or outer reality and the Imaginal or inner, archetypal, esoteric reality (shown at the top of the diagram).

story that involves a band of adventurers or a group of friends. There will always be a Leader, a Foil (called the Lancer on the TV Tropes page) who will be the opposite of the Leader, a Heart, being the character who is the most nurturing ,supportive, and healing, a Big Guy who is the warrior or the dumb muscle, and a Smart Guy, who is the opposite, the brains rather than the brawn.

Genre Tropes are what defines a story's universe or setting. Stories set in a particular genre have very specific tropes that set them apart from the other genres.

Some examples of genres might be high fantasy, urban fantasy, Space Opera, Cyberpunk, Steampunk, superhero, dystopian young adult, supernatural romance, and so on. In the broad sense, these genres are marketing pitches; readers or demographics like Tolkien might also like David Eddings, Robert Jordan, Brandon Sanderson, or Robin Hobbs. Or *World of Warcraft*, or *The Witcher*. Or *Dungeons & Dragons*, or *Runequest*, or *Warhammer*. Or they might not.

Storytellers incorporate these themes through watching or reading about them and then add them to their own stories. This is how culture builds upon earlier culture, with scientists and artists able to go further because they stand on the shoulders of giants – their predecessors.[79] An original story uses the tropes in a completely novel way, or even, although this rarely happens, introduces new tropes.

---

[79] As Isaac Newton wrote in 1675 in a letter to fellow scientist and polymath Robert Hooke: "If I have seen further it is by standing on the shoulders of Giants." The saying apparently goes back to twelfth-century French Neo-Platonist philosopher, scholar, and administrator Bernard of Chartres.

When overused, tropes can quickly become clichés, and stories are derivative and dull for this reason. But when used well, they introduce the reader to a universe that is already somewhat familiar, reducing the need for infodumps. Say "elf" for example, and one automatically thinks of a tallish, slender, refined, almost supernaturally beautiful, pale-skinned, pointy-eared humanoid race, with a deep spiritual bond with nature, who live in simple villages in forest glades, and whose choice of weapon is the bow, with which they are preternaturally skilled.

If one grew up in a culture without TV, movies, books, or storytellers, raised by wolves, so to speak, one would likely never come across any tropes (well, even there you would, but they would be wolves tropes). Tropes are almost entirely culture-dependent, although there can also be those who are based on individual experience. In any case, they come from the external and interpersonal world.

The ubiquitous nature of the trope across genres reveals its nature as a cultural or memetic expression of an Imaginal thoughtform, interfacing with the reader/viewer/listener through the medium of storytelling. This then creates a feedback loop, as both the creator and the reader/viewer/listener reinforce and further energize the trope/thoughtform/meme through the act of creative imagination on the part of the storyteller and creative or passive reception on the part of the reader/viewer/listener. Modern-day nerds, for example, are the equivalent of premodern religionists in that they dedicate energy to a particular thoughtform or story. The difference being that the nerd knows that the story is not objectively true, even as they participate in it through fandom, for example, whereas the religionist is living under the delusion that it is. This is the great contribution of modernity; it frees us from the collective slavery to religion.

Egotistic storytelling tropes tend to differ according to whether the writer is male or female. For example, a young adult female protagonist written by a male author may be characterized by superlative fighting ability, a strong sex life, and literally nothing else. No personality, no likes or dislikes in music, reading, or interest in shopping or make-up. The character may suddenly decide to be lesbian, or some other titillation or masturbatory fantasy the author may have. Conversely, a female author will eschew action and adventure and have a story where the protagonist has to overcome rivals for the attention of the male love interest, the ultimate aim being marriage and children. At that point, the story ends happily ever after.[80]

When storytelling departs from its mythopoetic and Imaginal roots, this sort of hack writing is the result.

The ultimate end result of banal, mundane ego-centered storytelling is to do without the story altogether and just film a bunch of people interacting, usually in a highly artificial setting in which emotional tensions are ramped up to provide drama because there is no story. Examples here are *Big Brother*, the *Bachelor/Bachelorette*, *Love Island*, and Mafs (*Married at First Sight*). If there is any excitement at all, it is only in having the hottest two contestants hook up. This shows such reality shows to be the dumbed-down versions of the already dumbed down

---

[80] See for example "Why are female characters written terribly??" by The Book Pusher, YouTube, 20 March, 2019 <https://youtu.be/E-ZM1ZqPnzM>.

and poorly written chick-lit or girlie stories in which, as mentioned, the whole aim of the story is for the female protagonist to overcome her rivals and get Mr. Right. Sometimes there's a love triangle, a choice between two Mr. Rights (*Twilight* et al.), or a Gary Stu Mr. Right and a psycho wannabe (*Fifty Shades* trilogy).

Other reality shows like *Survivor* involve celebrities, back-stabbing (called "playing the game"), and generally being totally amoral and manipulative.

All these reality shows are "people shows" with manufactured and hyped-up drama, overblown music, hyperbole in advertising, and so on.

## 19. FIVE TYPES OF NARRATIVE

lthough any number of types of narrative could be suggested, five can be distinguished here. These are the historical or factual Mundane (non-fiction), the Mundane-Personal (or personal mundane, a mix of factual and ego-fantasies), the Profane-Egoic (based on self-indulgent fantasies that generally reinforce the expectations of the lower emotional nature), the Mythic/Transpersonal, which is transitional between outer and inner being, and the revelatory visions of the esoteric or Imaginal world, which constitute the counterpole of the mundane world.

Popular works and genres represent the simplest form of narrative, lowbrow literature read for leisure, best sellers, airport novels, and beach reads, which require little effort to read and understand. The cinematic equivalent is the brainless blockbuster, and the computer games equivalent the first-person shooter and similar. Whatever the media, these are based on purely *Egoic* themes, totally profane and lacking in spiritual inspiration (indeed often the very antithesis of the Transpersonal, gnostic, and spiritual), often heavily stereotyped and cliched, and with only a smattering of historical and mythic elements. They result in cartoonish fantasies with no value other than indulging the ego in infantile fantasies and are very much big business in the mass media and entertainment industry, setting the standards for banal novels, "blockbuster" movies, and most video games.

Then there are more sophisticated, highbrow works of literature and film (or, to use simplistic categorization, "high-brow" literature and "art house" and "foreign" (continental European) cinema, which are more difficult to appreciate, and approach their characters from a more nuanced and realistic perspective. These provide a more nuanced approach to the personal and human existence, rather than gratifying the self-indulgent profane Ego. They thus contain far fewer clichés and more objective or historically factual elements. They can be called Mundane-Personal, in that, although they use personal and subjective imagination, they also take into account the realities of the mundane world. This includes adequately developed characters, complex interpersonal relationships, and real-life situations. The Egoic archetypes that so predominate profane fiction are here secondary and minimal, or even absent.

As a generalization, Egoic fiction tends to be represented by Hollywood's monolithic mass media machine, major publishers, and computer game producers. Mature fiction is represented by more sophisticated literature and independent media. Of course, these are not two distinctive categories but two poles within Profane-Egoic and Mundane-Personal storytelling.

## 20. THE PROFANE-EGOIC HERO/HEROINE

**B**ecause Profane-Egoic material is better known and easier to access and critique (especially by someone like me with little expertise in the classics), I will emphasize that in my coverage. For the sake of simplicity and my lack of knowledge in this field, I have focused on the Hollywood media machine and associated Western nations (Britain, Canada, Australia, etc.), and not considered rivals such as the vast Indian film industry jocularly designated as Bollywood (which actually puts out more films than Hollywood does). Of course, one could also focus on the profane and the mundane in other aspects of modern culture as well, such as education. In this way, Imaginal and Mythic studies can be used to provide a comprehensive integral analysis of the modern world. However, this is obviously far beyond the scope of the present essay.

The profane/Egoic imagination, and hence the characters and narratives of Egoic fiction, can be interpreted in terms of what Buddhists call the three *kleshas* (taints or poisons) of greed/lust, anger/hatred, and delusion/ignorance (*lobha*, *dosa*, *moha*). These are the three factors that determine *samsaric* existence (going around and around, replaying the same narrow loops in this and future lives) and keep us bound in our little world of separateness. Whereas the great myths trace archetypal-imaginative journeys of transformation, profane story-telling reinforces these attributes, and hence samsaric consciousness, with simplistic personal archetypes. These include Ego-ideal Hero (as Mundane-Personal rather than Imaginal myth and fantasy projection – hence "delusion"), Ego-fantasy Love Interest ("desire" or "lust," consider tropes as varied as the "hot librarian" and the "Bond girl," all represent examples of what a Jungian would call Anima-projection), and the Villain who represents everything bad (Shadow-projection). Hence, the reader has no qualms when the bad guy meets his comeuppance. Therefore, the hero has justified "anger" on the villain for killing innocent people or kidnapping his family, leading to the righteous vengeance plot, the opposite of teachings of authentic spirituality). Such pop-cultural story-telling rarely goes beyond the surface of emotional being (romantic and wish-fulfillment), mental being (primarily rational as in detective stories and science fiction), and the lower and most grotesque aspects of the astral (as in horror, crime, and other morbid subjects).

Ultimately, such a narrative focuses on an idealized image of the author's individual ego. Ian Fleming's super spy James Bond, for example, can be considered the classic male fantasy icon: dashing, elegant, irresistible to women, driving luxury sports cars, dodging bullets, beating up or killing innumerable bad guys (but only because they tried to kill him first), employing all kinds of incredible gizmos, and saving the world from supervillains. This cluster of Egoic wish-fulfillment elements has made the Bond franchise among the most successful in the modern world.

James Bond is unusual, however, in combining two very different aspects of Egoic male storytelling. Adopting the humanistic astrological archetypes of Dane Rudhyar and his school, these can be designated as Venusian and Martian (from Venus the goddess of Love and Mars the god of war). Intriguingly UFO contactee George Adamski's attractive or handsome "Nordic" aliens hailed from Venus, now known to be a toxic world incapable of supporting life (Adamski was tapping into the Imaginal myth, not the mundane scientific fact). On the Venusian side, the glamour and women, are represented with Hugh Hefner's playboy lifestyle. On the martial side are the cinematic action heroes played by John Wayne, Clint Eastwood, Steven Seagal, Bruce Willis, and other big stars, thriller writers such as Tom Clancy and Matthew Reilly. All cover similar ground to 007 but lack the glamorous ("Venus") protagonists and settings.

Often also with these action stories, the single hero is replaced by a band of heroes or anti-heroes, a *Dirty Dozen*, *Magnificent Seven*, *Oceans Eleven*, *A-Team*, or crew of the starship Enterprise, each with their archetypal qualities.[81] Each member of the team thus represents an aspect of the Ego or personality, the team as a whole representing the complete person. The better written of these move away from the Profane-Egoic to either the Mundane-Personal or the Mythic and even portray an important social message. An example here might be Gene Roddenberry's original *Star Trek* (debuting in 1966), which, in an age of

---

[81] See TV Tropes – Five Man Band <http://tvtropes.org/pmwiki/pmwiki.php/Main/FiveManBand> and numerous examples given therein. There does not have to be specifically five members; the original Star Trek features the three main protagonists of Captain Kirk, Mr Spock, and "Bones" McKoy, representing the Will, Reason, and Heart respectively (hence Rudolf Steiner's trilogy of thinking, feeling, and willing).

racism, sexism, and the cold war featured among the crew
a black woman (and the first television interracial kiss),
an Asian, a Russian, and an alien (Mr. Spock).

Most action fiction, sadly, is far less elevated. The Egoic
hero's only task, repeated *ad infinitum*, in literature,
cinema, television, and video game, is to trounce the
villain (who may be doing anything from hijacking a bus
or plane to threatening the world with nuclear weapons,
or in the case of the sci-fi hero, an alien creature or
fleet threatening the existence of human race) and thus
restore or maintain order. The Egoic hero is, in fact, the
symbol for the *yang* or aggressive, dominating polarity of
the Ego, which, to maintain its happy status (as limited
personality), has to constantly fend off attacks from the
subconscious, the Id, and the other. Indeed, this is pure
Freud. The Ego's entire existence is a titanic, constant
struggle, or succession of such struggles (as represented
symbolically by the villain or by a succession of villains),
in each of which it emerges victorious and hence
maintains its existence. The opposite to the state of the
Egoic hero is the transcendental or nondual Realisation
that there is no Ego, that ultimately this is all meaningless,
there is no struggle, nothing to fight against, but only a
surrendering into the Thatness or Suchness of existence as
it is. This is not something that can be represented in the
narrative. Hence even the lives of those who have attained
this state, such as Buddha and Jesus, are portrayed in
terms of standard mythic symbolism, obstacles, enemies,
betrayal, death and rebirth, etc.

So far, only the masculine polarity of the Ego in
storytelling has been described. But there are also female
equivalents in the romance narrative that go all the way
back Shakespeare's *Romeo and Juliet* – an authentic work

of mythopoesis which still unrivaled to this day and hence far above everything else discussed in this section – through the early classics of the Regency period such as Jane Austen's *Pride and Prejudice* (a sort of early 19th-century predecessor to the modern daytime soap opera), the Victorian period with the Bronte sisters (with novels such as *Jane Eyre* and *Wuthering Heights*, which deal with heavier themes than Austen does), during the twentieth century Margaret Mitchell's *Gone With the Wind* (the 1939 movie directed by Victor Fleming, starring Clark Gable and Vivien Leigh is sometimes considered the greatest movie ever made), and Barbara Cartland and the Mills & Boon publishing house, with others like Jackie Collins representing the more glamorous end of the spectrum. In the late 90s and the noughties, the female imagination was captured by *Sex and the City* franchise, based on a collection of essays by New York author and columnist Candace Bushnell which became a romantic drama television series, later adapted to a movie, deals with subjects such as sex, shopping, and relationships, but in the end, this tale of supposedly liberated and modern professional women falls flat with its protagonists obsessed only with finding Mr. Right, a fate as one dimensional as the action heroes repetitive thwarting of bad guys.

The "young adult" (to use marketing jargon) equivalent is somewhat more exotic, mixing school and growing up with vampire romance (although the vampire as a fantasy love interest is surely no more unrealistic than *Sex and the City 2*'s (2010) cartoonish portrayal of Middle Eastern culture). This genre culminates in Stephanie Myers' bestselling *Twilight* series. In Myers' emotionally gushy, first-person accounts, her protagonist Isabella Swan is the extreme passive female, weak and helpless and unable to do anything without her man, the diametric opposite of the extreme male stereotype. And it is also contrary to any strong female character, for example, Hermoine Granger of J. K. Rowling's equally popular (but more imaginative, even mythopoetic) *Harry Potter* mythos. Indeed, Bella's passivity has made her and her author the butt of numerous jokes and satires on internet discussion forums and YouTube videos, as well as putting an entire generation of nerds and geeks off vampires forever (hence the rise of the zombie as the rival Other). Yet although she does nothing but passively allows herself to be rescued by Byronesque vampire Edward Cullen, Bella is ironically still the one who holds all the cards in the *Twilight* mythos. This is because she has the power to choose between the two men who fight for her love, one a vampire and the other a werewolf (thus, *Twilight* represents one more example of the "monster mash"). In this instance, the extreme passive female becomes active, and the otherwise extreme male passive. Bella thus embodies the Egoic fantasies of numerous girls and women, just as Edward serves as a teen *Animus* projection.

Ironically, the theme in both franchises (*Sex and the City* and *Twilight*) is the same, just as the action movies are for men. It is all about filling stereotyped gender roles, with the female's only interest in finding true love, just as the male's only interest (in action movies) is fighting and blowing things up.

On another level, though, they constitute distinct Egoic-personal archetypes. In the terminology of humanistic astrology, the materialistic sex and shopping-obsessed crew of *Sex and the City* represent the glamour of Venus. In contrast, the ultra-passive Bella Swan of *Twilight* represents the Moon which can only reflect the light of its man (in this case, Edward as the sun around which Bella revolves); it cannot shine with its own light.

Ultimately, the passive, feminine Ego-polarity conquers through passivity. The choice of the object of desire is just as samsaric as the active male Ego-polarity that conquers through strength and aggression. They merely represent the opposite but complementary poles of the same psycho-physical structure, different aspects of the same *pingala* and *ida*, sympathetic and parasympathetic, waking and dreaming, willing and feeling, rationalism and imagination polarity already alluded to at the start of this essay. Both hyper-masculine and hyper-feminine serve as one-dimensional Egoic gender-stereotyped caricatures. Attempts at combining them to create more all-rounded characters are even worse, as shown by romantic comic book "sci-fi" movies like *Fantastic Four: The Rise of the Silver Surfer* (it's all about Sue's wedding), and *Spiderman 3* (it seems like everyone's crying all the time.[82])

At its best, such Profane-Egoic fiction provides escapist entertainment for the reader, regardless of whether it is action/thriller, romance, crime, sci-fi, or other genres. Yet all it does is provide escapism. It does not access the Imaginal World. It does not even access the Mythic/Transpersonal. There is no transformation of the consciousness of the reader or viewer and no "hero's journey." Especially when it is in the form of endless car chases, explosions, and, for example, vigilante plots (the bad guy commits a vicious crime, society fails to punish him, hero/heroine/victim takes things into their own hands), employing emotive tropes and distracting or stirring music.

---

[82] Why Part of *Spiderman 3* Sucks All That Crying! 27 Aug 2009. Uploaded by mlw8 <http://www.youtube.com/watch?v=7VIibC7oSK0>.

At its worst, however, Egoic fiction is nothing beyond the narcissistic wish-fulfillment fantasies of the author, satirized in fanfic (fiction written by fans of a particular television or movie franchise) as the "Mary Sue."[83] And while all authors incorporate Egoic fantasy elements in their fiction (the present writer not excluded), including characters who are sometimes too perfect to be accurate, the difference between a respectable although badly written or unrealistic character and a Mary Sue/Gary Stu seems to be that the accepted character is at the center of their mythos. In contrast, the Mary Sue in fanfic is a parasite who latches onto an already established mythos, such as *Star Trek* (in which fanfic the character of Mary Sue originally appears), and out-perfects even the perfect actions of the central protagonists of that mythos.

Either way, such banal entertainment takes advantage of all our lower emotion (vital *sensu* Sri Aurobindo) fantasies and impulses while providing very little, if anything, in the way of real inspiration or meaning. Yet ridiculous as such tropes often are, they are still necessary for reader or viewer identification. The mythopoeticist, therefore, must consider and incorporate some of the more important of both of these categories in his or her narrative. The more

---

[83] See e.g. Wikipedia <http://en.wikipedia.org/wiki/Mary_Sue> > and Television Tropes & Idioms <http://tvtropes.org/pmwiki/pmwiki. php/Main/MarySue>. Gary Stu and Ensign Jones are synonyms (Tee Morris, "Learning how to make your characters real" in Darin Park & Tom Dullemon, eds., *The Complete Guide to Writing Fantasy* vol.1: Alchemy with Words, Dragon Moon Press, 2002, pp.60-61). I was once told of an amusing instance of Mary Sue first hand. My brother used to meet with friends on a regular basis, for coffee and chat. A female acquaintance/friend who fancied herself a writer asked if she could come along. Being accepted on the condition that she did not write about them, she went to several of the get togethers, and then wrote a story featuring the others as they are, but herself as a beautiful concert violinist. I assume she wasn't invited to any more meetings!

faithfully and powerfully this is done, the more potent and memetic the resulting myth will be.

I have deliberately focused on only two forms of Profane-Egoic fiction, the hyper-masculine and hyper-feminine, to emphasize its basic themes. Often Profane-Egoic fiction may be more nuanced than this, and non-narcissistic Mundane-Personal fiction more so again. Nevertheless, what distinguishes personal from Mythic is that personal is grounded in this world and is about the human response to everyday things. In contrast, sci-fi and fantastical fiction (whether Profane-Egoic or Mundane-Personal) takes things of this world and transplants them into a distinct universe or mythos. True Mythic fiction adds various archetypal elements such as the hero's journey, the Other, Transformation, and Transcendence.

## 21. THE MYTHIC HERO

yths, by their very nature, are set in another world, another place, another time. It is a miraculous place, filled with larger-than-life characters, that constitutes the opposite to the dull and mundane world of everyday life. This Miraculous or Otherworldly setting means that the story takes place in the Imaginal World. It is a representation of the Imaginal, using familiar themes, people, and things that are juxtaposed into the surreal or dream-like. For example, the classic Western is purportedly set in a historical period of today's world but actually takes place in an idealized version of the late 19th century American Frontier. The Space Opera of *Star Trek* and *Star Wars* has nothing to do with actual rocket science but is set in an idealized universe where interstellar travel is ridiculously easy, and alien races and other planets take the same role that other countries and peoples have in history or today's world. Even serious, hard science writers like Asimov, Clarke, Heinlein, or Niven, have to resort to the *deus ex machina* of hyperspace or subspace jumps to get around the near-insurmountable difficulties of real star flight.[84] More

---

[84] Some idea of how difficult even near interplanetary spaceflight is can be seen by the American Government's recent cancellation of NASA's Ares rocket that was to return a man to the moon. Given current space technology, even a mission to Mars was looking increasingly

explicitly, the fantasy genre more explicitly emphasizes its otherworldly setting with reference to elves and orcs, magic, and dragons.

Even in a more purely Egoic sphere of writing, wish-fulfillment, genre restrictions, and the need for an uncomplicated narrative requires the way things are described is so unlike the world we know that it might as well take place on another planet or in a magical universe. Modern romances follow a stylized genre in which the various relationship conflicts and obstacles that provide narrative tension are always overcome in the happy ending, unlike real interpersonal relationships. In the world of action thrillers, jaundiced ex-cops can play vigilante heroes without worrying about the legal problems of actually having killed people, thus satisfying our sense of justice that is often thwarted when wrong-doers in real life get off lightly or not prosecuted at all. Marooned space travelers can rebuild a rocketship out of space junk. Detectives (too many examples to choose from, see the Wikipedia entry "Detective fiction") regularly solve problems that have the police stumped. Story-telling by its very nature takes one into an imaginary world, and this goes double and triple for television, cinema, and computer games, with their immersive quality.

But thrillers and cop shows aside, it is the genre variously referred to in literature as "science fiction and fantasy,"

unlikely, at least until Elon Musk came along. For a more optimistic look at Interplanetary Travel, see Duncan Lunan, *Man and the Planets: The Resources of the Solar System*, Ashgrove Press, Bath, 1983. For a good study of real Interstellar flight, see Eugene Mallove and Gregory Matloff, *The Starflight Handbook: A Pioneer's Guide to Interstellar Travel*, John Wiley & Sons, 1989.

Fantastical Fiction, or Speculative Fiction,[85] is always for me the one that serves as a particularly rich medium for mythopoesis.

The archetype of the hero/heroine differs markedly, according to the degree of inwardness of consciousness the author accesses. The most significant distinction is between the Egoic hero/heroine, which constitutes most contemporary and pop-cultural entertainment, and the Transpersonal or Mythic hero/heroine. The difference between the two is that the former serves as narcissistic gratification of the lower emotional being of both the author and the reader/viewer, whereas the latter is genuinely transformative. Obviously, there is a lot of cross-over between these two types.

Authentic mythopoesis accesses the Imaginal World either through universal symbolism, direct experience, or both. The Mythic hero or heroine thus involves authentic archetypal themes of the hero's journey, transformation, death, and resurrection, even if this is portrayed in strongly anthropomorphic symbolism. Although usually associated with traditional archetypes represented by figures of classic mythology and traditional religion, there are many instances today when mythopoeticists are able to directly access and embody universal, rather than merely personal, themes. For example, Tolkien's Middle Earth mythos or George Lucas' original *Star Wars* trilogy

---

[85] Speculative fiction is an umbrella story-telling genre generally encompassing the more specific genres of science fiction, fantasy, horror, supernatural story-telling, superhero story-telling, utopian and dystopian story-telling, apocalyptic and post-apocalyptic story-telling, and alternate history – Belinda Henwood, *Publishing*. Career FAQs Pty Ltd. 2007, p. 86 – cited in Wikipedia, Speculative fiction. Obviously, many classic mythologies and epics could easily be said to fall within this category were they written today.

have equal power to awe and inspire as any religious or metaphysical treatise. The only difference between some of these "premodern" epics and those of the modern world is that those associated with religions were considered historically and even metaphysically accurate and sacred.

The Mythic hero or heroine may be quite variable, even within a single mythos. Compare, for example, the two types of the male hero, the child-like Frodo and the warrior Aragorn, of Tolkien's Lord of the Rings. On the other hand, they would seem to find very close counterparts in the two very different types of female protagonists – ten-year-old Chihiro Ogino of *Spirited Away* and the eponymous warrior Princess Mononoko in Japanese anime writer-director Hayao Miyazaki's works. And in contrast to the Egoic hero, the Mythic hero does not have to be a surrogate for the author, although inevitably, some degree of "author avatar" is unavoidable.

Although many Mythic themes could be considered, two seem to be of primary importance: the Hero's Journey of transformation and apocalyptic transcendence. The former is found in the old, cyclic *Myth of the Hero* (Joseph Campbell, J. R. R. Tolkien) characterized by traditionalism, premodernism, and a cyclic cosmology (following Tolkien, most fantasy epics take place in a pseudo-medieval setting, although this is not the case with modern adaptations such as the Harry Potter series, which are based on the English Private School system). The latter represents Egoic transcendence of individuality and hence even the Mythic hero/heroine (as a symbol of the Imaginal Self) in a higher reality, but external forms of exoteric religious apocalypticism distort this occult and spiritual principle.

In cyclic cosmology, the hero's role is to restore and renew the world to its romantic ideal, rather than to radically change it, even though the hero is radically transformed in the process, sometimes undergoing sacrificial death and rebirth (as in the classic Christ mythos). Popular examples here include Frodo and Aragorn in Tolkien's *Lord of the Rings* (in many ways the origin of the entire high fantasy genre – see Peter Jackson's magnificent film adaptation), Luke Skywalker in George Lucas' *Star Wars* trilogy (a reinventing of the classic Space Opera), the eponymous Harry Potter in J. K. Rowling's seven-volume series, Neo in the Walchalskis' *Matrix* trilogy (the latter two *Matrix* films, unfortunately, were not received well, perhaps due to their intellectual and Mythic themes, although the ridiculous unarmoured exoskeletons of the climactic battle scene didn't help), Maximus Decimus Merdius in *Gladiator*, Kaitniss Everdeen in *Hunger Games*, the eponymous Mandalorian in the Disney/*Star Wars* Space Western of the same name, and many others."

The incredibly powerful, even timeless, Mythic trope of the hero or superhero, the protector who comes out of nowhere to save innocents from a heartless evil threat or antagonist, pitting good and against evil to save the day, is beautifully presented by Welsh singer Bonnie Tyler's hit 1984 single, "Holding Out For A Hero," a song that transcends its original romantic context, having been given numerous presentations on YouTube with footage from Marvel, DC, and other heroes and superheroes.

## 22. THE END OF THE MAGICAL AGE

any epic mythoi seem to describe the end of the age of Magic and Myth. Although Tolkien's Fellowship managed to defeat Sauron by destroying the ring, the story (and the Third Age of Middle Earth) ends on a sad note, with Frodo, Gandalf, and others leaving Middle Earth for the Undying Lands across the sea to the West (clearly inspired by the Greek Elysian Fields, the final resting places of the souls of the virtuous, the Norse Valhalla, the abode of slain heroes, and the Irish Tír na nÓg[86]; obviously these are three representations of the Imaginal afterlife). By the time of the "Fourth Age," they had been joined by almost all of the elves, while hobbits, although present, are fewer in numbers, more diminutive in stature, reclusive, and hard to find. Other nonhuman races likewise declined. As with the Indian *Mahabharata,* there is a great battle in which

---

[86] From Wikipedia: "Tír na nÓg was considered a place beyond the edges of the map, located on an island far to the west. It could be reached by either an arduous voyage or an invitation from one of its fairy residents. The isle was visited by various Irish heroes and monks in the *echtrae* (Adventure) and *immram* (Voyage) tales popular during the Middle Ages. This otherworld was a place where sickness and death do not exist. It was a place of eternal youth and beauty. Here, music, strength, life, and all pleasurable pursuits came together in a single place. Here happiness lasted forever; no one wanted for food or drink."

the "good guys" are victorious. Yet, rather than restoring the golden age, it ushers in the Kali Yuga (in Hindu cosmology), which is not so much a "dark age" as a period of materialism and blandness – with the elves gone, magic also vanishes from the world. All that remains then is Steiner's Ahriman, the skeptical-materialistic mindset. Therefore, such myths symbolize the involution, descent, or incarnation of consciousness from the Imaginal to the material-physical.

Also of mention here is George Lucas' *Star Wars*, in which the fairy tale beginning "a long time ago in a galaxy far far away" places the *Star Wars* universe in the mythic past, with no relation to the mundane world of here and now, with the battle of the rebels against the empire equivalent to the epic battles in the *Mahabharata* and the *Lord of the Rings*. And just as elves and hobbits disappear from Middle Earth, while men (representing the mundane world, after all, how many hobbits do you see running around today?[87]) grow more numerous, in the original *Star Wars* trilogy, Obi One Kenobi, Darth Vader, Yoda, and finally Luke Skywalker are the last remaining Jedi.[88]

Symbolically then, Tolkien's Third Age, and the events of the *Mahabharata* (including the birth, life, and death of

---

[87] Ironically an extinct species of tiny prehistoric hominid – an example of Island Dwarfism – found on the Island of Flores in Indonesia (*Homo floresiensis*) was named "the hobbit".

[88] The Sith as the evil counterpart of the Jedi are not mentioned until the prequel trilogy, beginning with *The Phantom Menace* in 1999. The word itself does appear in a revised rough draft for the original movie, but never made it on screen (When did the Sith enter the *Star Wars* canon?, Science Fiction & Fantasy Stack Exchange <https://scifi.stackexchange.com/questions/7529/when-did-the-sith-enter-the-star-wars-canon>).

Krishna and the great battle on the field of Kurukshetra), both symbolize the transitional dramaturgic events between the Imaginal origin, the Dreamtime (to use the very appropriate Australian Aboriginal terminology), or what mythographer and gnostic scholar Mircea Eliade's sacred origin located *in illo tempore* (in mythical time), and the world of history, time, space, and causation in which we find ourselves. This same progressive loss of paradise is also found in Steiner's cosmology of Root Races and culture epochs, notably the transition from the Atlantean to the present, Post-Atlantean era. In Theosophy, Anthroposophy, and New Age cosmology, the destruction of Atlantis fills the same role as the respective battles in the *Mahabharata* and the *Lord of the Rings*. Whether this refers to an actual cosmological (but supra-physical and mytho-historical) event in the Imaginal World (like the pre-creation crisis in Gnosticism and Lurianic Kabbalah), or simply the transition from a supra-physical to a constricted material existence in individual incarnation, confusion of both, or other factors not considered here, I cannot at this time say.

## 23. FROM HERO TO ANTI-HERO

Although the archetypes of the Imaginal World are timeless and non-evolutionary, once they interact with the individual and socio-cultural human dimensions, they are drawn into the world of time and space, and hence of history. It is therefore not possible to speak of eternal Platonic forms within the mundane realm. As long as one has a body and is part of history and "the terrestrial evolution" (to use Sri Aurobindo's term for spiritual evolution in the material world), there is change and transformation.

We find this with myths as well. For the sake of convenience, I will focus only on the type of contemporary myth as it appears in print and cinema.

The metamorphosis of the Cowboy begins with the traditional cowboy-hero-outsider. Perhaps the most evocative representation of this archetype-trope is George Stevens' 1953 movie *Shane*, based on a novel of the same name by Jack Schaefer, and starring Alan Ladd in the title role. This represents the Classic Western Plot (*sensu* Will Wright *Sixguns and Society*) with the Christ-like premodern hero who appears out of nowhere (the wilderness, the unknown). Reluctantly drawn into the conflict against the villainous cattle barons, he saves the homestead family and then rides out to disappear into the desert from whence he came. His high principled idealism and strong pacifism represent conservative society and Christian-based moral ideals before the 60s revolution of social mores.

Later movies such as Sergio Leone's epic 1966 spaghetti Western *The Good the Bad and the Ugly* (starring Clint Eastwood) and George Roy Hill's 1969 *Butch Cassidy and the Sundance Kid* (with Paul Newman and Robert Redford), feature the mercenary gunslinger or outlaw anti-hero. This represents the Professional Western Plot (*sensu* Will Wright). It reflects the world of late 20th-century capitalist modernity, where it's every man for himself and where profit and adventure rather than high principles are the order of the day.

As the Wild West receded into historical irrelevance, its place has been taken by the desolation of a lawless post-apocalyptic future. Yet, although the Post-apocalyptic hero lives in the future, he is an identical figure to the cowboy gunslinger of the past for all intents and purposes. Past and future are just arbitrary referents, symbolic of the *otherness* of the Imaginal World, a place that is not here, not part of the mundane world of historical space and time in which we exist on a material rational-skeptical level.

The traditional Post-apocalyptic hero is represented by Max Rockatansky (played by Mel Gibson) in George Miller's 1981 epic *Mad Max II The Road Warrior*. Here is a reluctant Shane-like savior figure who appears from nowhere at the start of the narrative and disappears back into the wilderness from whence he came once his task is complete. Instead of riding a horse, he drives a car, although not an ordinary car, but a numinous, Imaginal one, "the last of the V-8 Interceptors", black, battered, and supercharged, with banks of exhausts and air vents (an exact replica can be found outside the hotel in Silverton, outback NSW, where the movie was filmed). The influence of this movie is so great (in relation to the little-known prequel and disappointing sequel) that it could be said to have single-handedly established the post-apocalyptic genre in the popular imagination.

Later on, the post-apocalyptic hero appears as the restorer of civilization, represented by David Brin's 1985 science fiction novel *The Postman* and Kevin Costner's 1997 film adaptation. Here the post-apocalyptic hero does not return to the desert but rather is actively involved in recreating civilization. A very different example, this time with a rejection of modernity and postmodernity and more explicate Christian religious overtones, is Albert and Allen Hughes 2010 movie *The Book of Eli* starring Denzel Washington, and implausibly is based on the idea of all the world's bibles being destroyed bar one—symbolic of exoteric religious insecurity in the face of modernity—which is necessary to restore civilization.

The pattern of transition from altruistic to cynical cowboy is mirrored in the transition of comic book superheroes from modernity to post-modernity. Batman's transformation from a crime-fighting hero to the Dark Knight anti-hero, or the traditional values of the JLA, and the darker, edgier Watchmen, is comparable to the traditional morality of the 1940-60s being replaced by the postmodern nihilism of the late 80s, 90s, and noughties. In these cases, we are dealing not with the Hero on the Universal/Mythic level, but with the personal level of story-telling, in which myths are used as commentary on social issues.

## 24. SCIENCE FICTION AS MODERN-DAY MYTHOLOGY

If the novel is the individual — rather than the tribe, the culture, or the society — as the locus of mythopoesis and story-telling, then science fiction is that same individualization representing the most fundamental characteristics of Modernity: the arc of progress. History is no longer a fall, or even a progressive degradation, from an original paradise or golden age, or an endless series of unchanging cycles, as in traditional mythopoesis, but an upward ascent to greater complexity and development. This new archetype, or transtype, dates from the late 18th century onwards.[89]

---

[89] The scientific and evolutionary perspective of the cosmos is the convergence of a number of discoveries. In 1796 the French mathematician and scientist Pierre-Simon Laplace developed a naturalistic version of Swedish scientist and mystic Emanuel Swedenborg's and German philosopher Immanuel Kant's nebular hypothesis for the origin of the Solar System, as well as describing celestial mechanics, although his famous reply to Napoleon when queried regarding the role of God – "I have no need of that hypothesis," seems to have been apocryphal. Shortly after, the French zoologist Jean-Baptiste Lamarck in 1809 published the – unpopular at the time – theory that organisms change through time. The actual mechanism of the evolution of life was developed independently into empirical theory by Charles Darwin and Alfred Russel Wallace, and expanded in detail by Darwin's *On the Origin of Species* in 1859. In the 20th century, all these and other cosmological, geological, biological, and sociological

Science fiction had its precursors in fantastical stories from classic, medieval, and early modern times, including the Roman satirist Lucian's *A True Story* (2nd century C.E.), some elements of *The Arabian Nights*, Cyrano de Bergerac's stories, and Jonathan Swift's *Gulliver's Travels* (1726). However, English science fiction writer Brian Aldiss dates the beginning of science fiction to Mary Shelley's Gothic horror story *Frankenstein* (1818).[90] French writer Jules Verne (1828-1905) is a better candidate for his *Journey to the Center of the Earth* (1864), *From the Earth to the Moon* (1865), and *Twenty Thousand Leagues Under the Sea* (1870), all of which, while dated now, incorporated the hard science of his time. After Verne, English author H. G. Wells (1866-1946) next best qualifies as the father of modern science fiction, with works like *The Time Machine* (1895), *The Island of Doctor Moreau* (1896), *The Invisible Man* (1897), and *The War of the Worlds* (1898), and *The First Men in the Moon* (1901). He covered such classic topics as alien invasions, biological engineering, invisibility, space travel, and time travel.

The following decades featured planetary romances and pulp stories about mad scientists and robots. The movie franchise *Star Wars*, for example, is better understood as a throwback to the Age of Pulps and *Flash Gordon* than to true science fiction.

But it was in 1937, when John W. Campbell became editor of *Astounding Science Fiction*, that science fiction in the

---

evolution all converged in the scientific idea of the material universe as evolving towards greater complexity. This worldview of a progressive universe defined by natural laws replaced the premodern creationist model of an external deity.

[90] Brian Aldiss, *Billion Year Spree*, Doubleday, 1973.

modern sense began, with writers like Isaac Asimov, Arthur C Clarke, Robert Heinlein, A. E. Van Vogt, Theodore Sturgeon, and others. When I was a kid growing up and reading my father's science fiction paperbacks and books he borrowed from the local library, this was the type of science fiction I absorbed. This is very much along the lines of the "hard" or realistic science fiction genre.

1950s movies like *The Day the Earth Stood Still*, and especially the classic *Forbidden Planet*, are examples of this genre. In the mid-1960s, Gene Roddenberry's *Star Trek*, with its utopian optimism, is based on this classic Golden Age science fiction.

Following this Golden Age of the 40s through to the early 60s, there was a reaction against dry sensation-thinking orientated story-telling, with the more feeling-orientated and humanistic, literary, New Wave stories of the 60s and 70s. Stanisław Lem (*Solaris*), Frank Herbert (*Dune*), Philip K. Dick, and feminist and anthropological science fiction writer Ursula K. Le Guin are representative of this period.

The 80s and 90s saw genres like Cyberpunk, inspired by rampant capitalism and the information age culture, as well as various military science fiction stories. In the early 21st-century science fiction include environmental issues, biotechnology, nanotechnology, post-scarcity societies, and often more realistic stories (given the tremendous challenges of interstellar travel) set in this solar system or even just on Earth. At the same time, however, space opera, galactic empire-style science fantasy, continues to be a popular genre.

Despite its exoteric, non-gnostic, gross physical emphasis — the surrealist-paranoid gnostic writer Philip K. Dick being perhaps the only exception here, just as H. P. Lovecraft is the only real visionary in horror fiction — science fiction remains an important instrument of the imagination. Like all speculative/imaginative story-telling, science fiction is a way of approaching and presenting the Imaginal World, using the language and concepts of secular Modernity.

Whereas for fantasy worlds, the rationalist skepticism of waking consciousness brings the negation, the cold hard light of day in which dreams and imaginings are shown to be just that, fantasy, with no grounding in the material world, science fiction embraces this very rationalism and modernity, to create new mythoi of transcendence from it. Science fiction tends to focus on social commentary and problem solving within fictional settings. As social commentary, science fiction is very much about the modern, historical world. And the sub-genre of hard science fiction serves as a venue for speculation on the social impact of futuristic yet sometimes entirely plausible technologies, such as genetic engineering, nanotech, artificial intelligence, and space exploration.

This sort of rationalistic science fiction has no real commonality with fantasy or the more traditional mythopoetics, which pertain to the Hero's Journey. Instead, it emphasizes the technological speculation of rational secular consciousness. It does not deny magic but subsumes it under technology, in the form of Arthur C. Clarke's famous "third law" of prediction, "Any sufficiently advanced technology is indistinguishable from magic." From a gnostic or an occult perspective, that is a meaningless statement because authentic magic occurs on an Imaginal, metaphysical plane of existence and has nothing to do with technology, advanced or otherwise.

Yet intriguingly and paradoxically, hard science fiction technologies, certainly possible given continued technological progress (assuming civilization doesn't implode or enter a new dark age through resource depletion, environmental destruction, or other factors), also have an Imaginal aspect, by their sheer strangeness relative to our current collective Egoic and Mythic perspective.

The fact that hard science fiction focuses on the rational mundane consciousness does not mean it lacks narrative or character development, and what distinguishes science fiction is precisely that it includes these things. But it does differ in that it proposes a forward-looking perspective in contrast to the neo-medieval romanticism of high fantasy. Science fiction writer David Brin, for example, is very critical of mythic-cyclic stories of Tolkien and Lucas.[91] From the perspective of the cultural-evolutionary stages described by writers like Ken Wilber and, following him, Steve McIntosh,[92] this is an example of "culture war" (or clash of ideas) – the Traditional (fantasy/ science fantasy) vs. the Modern (science fiction) (also compare neo-Sufi Traditionalism versus syncretic "New Age" in esotericism). This raises questions regarding

---

[91] David Brin and Matthew Woodring Stover, *Star Wars on Trial: Science Fiction and Fantasy Writers Debate the Most Popular Science Fiction Films of All Time*, BenBella Books, Inc., 2006.

[92] Wilber *Up From Eden* and subsequent works, especially *A Theory of Everything*, based on the Spiral Dynamics material of Don Beck and Chris Cowan, and McIntosh *Integral Consciousness and the Future of Evolution*, which is probably more loyal to the Spiral Dynamics of Clare Graves, Don Beck, and Chris Cowan than Wilber is.

the relationship between Mythic narratives and the contemporary world and how such narratives embody particular historical social structures or ethical systems. This is all part of the role of science fiction, to question and comment from a rational perspective, in contrast to fantasy, which is all about immersion in a romantic world of the imagination.

Of the various genres of science fiction, Space Opera is simply the revisioning of original myths and fairy tales, with larger than life characters and absurd story-telling, representing specific cultural tropes and personality psychotypes[93] and archetypes. Unlike other types of science fiction, Space Opera is not about the present or the future, but the past. The similarity with premodern myths is because it shares the same function – the same with superheroes.

The Space Opera style of science fiction, and related speculative genres such as high and urban fantasy, superheroes, and supernatural romance, are the modern-day equivalents of classic mythology, complete with heroes and villains, gods and monsters (or aliens and supervillains), escapism, and social commentary, all dressed up in the tropes and themes of the modern world.

---

[93] The "psychotype" is not a dynamic primordial Jungian symbol of transformation ("archetypes"), but a more static, premodern myth-inspired typology, such as described by American psychologist James Hillman, who broke with Jung's analytical school to develop his own Archetypal Psychology based on archetypes as Imaginal motifs like polytheistic gods; author and educator Carol S. Pearson, who along with psychologist Hugh Marr developed a system of self-inquiry based on twelve universal Archetypes, and psychiatrist and Jungian analyst of Jean Bolen, author of *Goddesses in Everywoman: A New Psychology of Women* (1984) and *Gods in Everyman: A New Psychology of Men's Lives and Loves*, (1989).

In addition to Space Opera, there are various other subgenres: Cyberpunk, Steampunk, time-travel, alternate history, post-apocalyptic, but with the exception of the near-future setting Cyberpunk, none of these are specifically futurism-orientated mythopoesis. Even post-apocalyptic is about the modern world, but if a catastrophe (zombies, alien invasion, catastrophic climate change) had to bring about the end of civilization, leaving the protagonists free to explore an environmentally inhospitable, amoral, and lawless barbarian world.

Regarding intelligent, high concept, science fiction, the two most characteristic types are hard and soft or social science fiction, referring to the hard sciences (astronomy, physics, etc.) and the soft or social or human sciences (anthropology, sociology, etc.) that each type addresses

Hard science fiction is all about problem-solving. There is often little in the way of character arcs, story-telling, or worldbuilding, although there are some exceptions here. One example is Andy Weir's 2011 novel *The Martian*. Weir's astronaut has to use his knowledge of science to meet the challenges of surviving on his own on Mars. Or Liu Cixin's 2008 *The Three-Body Problem*, about a threatened invasion of Earth by an alien race, the Trisolarians, whose solar system includes three suns orbiting each other in an unstable three-body system (referring to the three-body problem in orbital mechanics).

Social science fiction, instead of solving technical or scientific challenges, considers social, etc. Ursula K. Le Guin's 1968 best-selling science fiction novel *The Left Hand of Darkness* explores the culture and society of a race of asexual humanoid aliens, who only adopt sexual characteristics once a month, during which they can equally become male or female. This scenario allows Le Guin to explore what society could be like without gender or the constant pressure of sexuality and sexual relationships.

Novels such as *The Left Hand of Darkness*, although works of speculative fiction that may feature classic tropes such as interstellar travel, are not about the future, or even (as with fantasy) the past, but the present. The purpose of elaborate worldbuilding is to provide a hypothetical universe in which society and the human condition can be examined free from current historical, social, or biological constraints.

The combination of Space Opera, hard science fiction, and social science fiction has led to the creation of future histories. These serve the same function as old mythological histories of premodern societies like Homeric and Hesiodic Greece, the post-exilic Old Testament history of the Hebrews, and Hindu epics like the *Ramayana* and *Mahabharata*, except that they are set in the future rather than the past, giving Imaginal meaning through looking forward to a world to come, rather than a past Golden Age.

The first of these epic stories, and the one that set the standard that all the others would follow, was Isaac Asimov's *Foundation* series, the writing of the first part of which dates to 1941, with the complete trilogy published in their final form from 1951 to 1953. This work of future history covers the efforts of mathematician Hari Seldon and the Encyclopedists to stave off a dark age that will last thirty thousand years, shortening it to a mere millennium. While written from the rational-modern perspective of hard science fiction, and inspired by Edward Gibbon's *The History of the Decline and Fall of the Roman Empire*, its epic, galaxy-spanning scale is surely Mythic and Imaginal in scope, but a mythology of the future, rather than the past, based on the plot device of an imaginary deterministic branch of mathematics and statistic called Psychohistory. Psychohistory becomes a new trope, a Transtype looking back from the future rather than a religious and anthropomorphic deity from the mythic tradition and racial memory of the past. Even Hari Seldon, the story's unlikely intellectual protagonist, only appears at the start of the thousand-year narrative, later being replaced by successors, although appearing every so often as a hologram to advise his successors.

The mythopoetic rationalism of *Foundation* made it the first true Space Opera. From *Foundation* came countless derivatives, some good, others less so, including both the serious worldbuilding and millennium-spanning galactic history of Frank Herbert's *Dune* series, perhaps the only science-fiction epic to equal *Foundation* in scope of imagination, as well as Gene Roddenberry's *Star Trek* with its utopian interstellar Federation, and, building on all these and more, the matinee popcorn *Flash Gordon* style of the Star Wars series, itself owing a large debt of inspiration and worldbuilding tropes to *Foundation*, including a city planet, aircars, spaceships that travel faster than light through hyperspace, a fall of Rome scenario, and a galaxy-spanning empire.

The romantic quality of science fiction, especially of the more popular "Space Opera" type, is that it is everyday story-telling set in a mythopoetic future among the stars. It could equally be a thriller, a romance, a western, a detective story, an adventure story, a soap opera, except that it is set in a futuristic setting. Here, the value of the story, exactly as with fantasy, romance, or any other genre, lies in transporting the reader to a new life, a world of the imagination, as a distraction from their everyday humdrum existence. The story does not have to be sophisticated, as it serves no didactic purpose, only entertainment.

Related to science fiction, but without the narrative fiction devices of plot and character, and often set over vast time spans, are actual future histories. First and foremost was the British philosopher and science fiction author Olaf Stapledon, whose *Last and First Men: A Story of the Near and Far Future*, describes the evolution of humanity from the present day to two billion years in the future.

Among Scottish science writer Dougal Dixon's prolific output is his 1990 *Man After Man: An Anthropology of the Future*, which explores a hypothetical future human evolution from 200 years to 5 million years in the future, including many truly bizarre species. This work, and *First and Last Men*, was obviously the inspiration for Turkish artist and author C. M. Kosemen (pseudonym Nemo Ramjet) extraordinary 2006 work of speculative future evolution, *All Tomorrows: A Billion Year Chronicle of the Myriad Species and Mixed Fortunes of Man,* which explores future humans and their descendants over a billion years of galactic evolution and featuring surreal artwork that helps convey the sense of an Imaginal future across deep time.

| | Backward tending - to a nostalgic/ mythical past | Set in the present day | Forward oriented, to a future interplanetary or interstellar empire |
|---|---|---|---|
| Larger than life, sometimes ridiculously so (Mythic / Traditional) | Religious myths, some classical myths | Superhero, swashbuckling, popcorn matinee movies | Space Opera (e.g. Star Wars and similar) |
| Epic stories, but not so extreme as to appear unrealistic | Lord of the Rings | Genre stories (adventure, romance, etc) | Foundation, Dune |
| True to life within the genre or setting (Rational-Modernity) | Some modern fantasy perhaps? | Noir fiction, gritty realism, true to life romance | Hard science fiction; Social science fiction |

*Table 1.* Types of fantastical fiction. The categories and examples are purely for illustration, and not intended as absolute categories.

## 25. SCIENCE FICTION VERSUS FANTASY

In discussing science fiction and fantasy in cinema and literature, there is sometimes the distinction between science fiction as a literary genre, generally represented by the capitalized initials SF, and the much less rigorous, and often very much more poorly written, grand ideas wise, science fiction of television and cinema. This latter is referred to as "sci-fi" (rhymes with hi-fi) and is generally looked on with disgust by serious SF writers. Sci-fi is not so much SF as a sort of amorphous mixture of SF, fantasy, and horror, often written in a formulaic way or dumbed down and diluted due to constant rewrites of the original screenplay. This is precisely the reason for the qualitative superiority of written text over the cinematic medium. The written text is the work of one individual who can present their creativity pure. Nevertheless, in rare instances, a director is able to create his own vision unhindered or present a very good adaptation of a written work. Hence these works tend to be epic indeed. *Metropolis, 2001 A Space Odyssey, Star Wars, The Matrix, Lord of the Rings,* and *Avatar* are some examples – as are the Japanese anime, including the works of Hayao Miyazaki (*Spirited Away, Princess Mononoke, Howl's Moving Castle,* and many others), Hideaki Anno (*Neon Genesis Evangelion*), Tetsurō Araki (*Attack on Titan, Death Note*). Katsuhiro Otomo

(*Akira*), Mamoru Oshii (*Ghost in the Shell*) – of the more pre-eminent. Independent film producers and directors have the same creative freedom, but not the vast budgets required to create a contemporary blockbuster.

Although modern fantastical story-telling dates from the 19th and turn of the 20th century, century, with authors such as Mary Woolstonecraft Shelley, Jules Verne, Bram Stoker, and H.G. Wells, its counterparts can be found in epic works of classic mythology such as Homer's *Odyssey* or tales of Jason and the Argonauts, which feature travels to travels to new lands, encounters with fantastical creatures, and so on. Even 18th-century satire, as with Jonathon Swift's *Gulliver's Travels*, represents a work that by all intents and purposes was the science fiction story of its day (a lone adventurer travels to unknown islands (worlds) and encounters strange people and creatures (aliens)).

Science fiction and fantasy can be distinguished and contrasted in the same way that skeptical reason and intuitive imagination are. Science fiction uses speculation from science and technology, whereas fantasy employs magic and creates worlds not bound by the laws of physics as we know them.[94] Nevertheless, fantasy worlds still have to be consistent regarding their laws of how magic works.

While it is easy to distinguish between two types of fantastical settings — the futuristic, high-tech universes of *Star Trek* and the medieval-like universe of Tolkien's Middle Earth, for example — often the lines between

---

[94] Darin Park, "Forward", in Darin Park & Tom Dullemon, eds., *The Complete Guide to Writing Fantasy vol.1: Alchemy with Words*, Dragon Moon Press, 2002, pp.7-8.

science fiction and fantasy are not clearly defined. Many people, for example, think of *Star Wars* as science fiction. However, it is best described as science fantasy, in that along with spaceships and ray guns, it also incorporates mystical elements such as the Force and Jedi Knights. These mystical elements are precisely what gives the *Star Wars* mythos its power, so it is a pity that Lucas would damage the mystique of his original trilogy in his disappointing later prequels, in which the Force is explained materialistically via "midichlorians," which for me all but destroyed the Mythic grandeur of the *Star Wars* universe. Indeed, most of the better-known science fiction universes (mythoi) certainly include both.[95]

While science fiction and fantasy are natural opposites and complements, what is interesting and perhaps reflective of the morbid and grotesque state of the ordinary human imagination, is that there is no popular genre that is the counter-pole of horror. Now, to me, the logical opposite of horror, of stories about demons and monsters, would be tales of angelic beings and miracles. Although the New Age movement might fill that role, this is a movement, not a literary genre. The quality of New Age novels is also questionable. Admittedly the only one I have attempted to read has been the excruciatingly poorly written *Celestine Prophecy*. So, as the opposite of horror, I would suggest a fourth genre of fantastical story-telling, which is Transcendence.

Fantastical story-telling thus may include all four elements but differ as to their proportion or emphasis.

---

[95] Charlie Jane Anders The greatest SF universes that include both magic and science fiction. <http://io9.com/5555751/12-sf-universes-that-include-magic-and-science-fiction> (Retrieved 6 June 2010). With a little googling, many similar lists could easily be found.

So transcendent story-telling generally always features stories of battle with monsters but differs from horror in that these have a less overbearing role to play in the story, or that the two sides are more evenly matched so that in the end, the Darkness is vanquished by the Light.

## 26. ENCOUNTER WITH THE OTHER

**M**eeting the Imaginal could be described as meeting The Other. The Imaginal and the Unconscious Psyche that it appears through are so different to the Ego and its mundane personality that it appears totally alien and Other.

The Other is a denizen of psychology and myth (and hence ultimately of the Imaginal World) that differs from the villain of Egoic or personal mythology. It embodies a genuine sense of alienness and the uncanny. Because of this, the Other may be assimilated with the Shadow to take frightening or monstrous form. However, the Other can appear as beautiful and numinous as well, for example, the royal elf Galadriel of Tolkien's Middle Earth mythos.

It is, however, the frightening Other that is the more popular, or perhaps simply because it is easier to represent, in popular fiction. Of note especially are the stop-motion animation Ray Harryhausen, an American film producer, and a special effects creator. The creatures he conjures up in *Jason and the Argonauts*, *Sinbad*, and other such movies[96] are far more evocative than the

---

[96] See for example Harryhausen's *The 7th Voyage of Sinbad* (1958),

smoother movement of CGI monsters in contemporary blockbusters. Their jerky nature adds a surreal element that adds to the awe and terror of encounters with strange creatures and battles with monsters. This sensation is simply not there in modern special effects, where the monsters and superheroes tend to appear as ridiculous and hence non-threatening.

Just as the Hero undergoes a transformation in the socio-cultural evolution of Egoic and mythopoetic storytelling, so does the Other. Two examples of this are Other into Hero, and Shadow into *Animus*.

James Cameron's Terminator franchise begins (with the 1984 *The Terminator*) with the Other as a monstrous machine, the Terminator robot (played by Arnold Schwarzenegger), which is sent back in time to kill Sarah Connor, the mother of John Connor, the human resistance leader in the battle against the evil machines. The plan is only thwarted when a human soldier, Kyle Reese, is sent back to protect Sarah. The 1991 sequel *Terminator 2: Judgment Day* sees the transformation of Other to Hero, as the Terminator robot has taken Kyle's role as protector of John Connor and the human race against the sinister liquid metal T-1000. In the final scene, he sacrifices himself like a Wagnerian hero so that the chip in his brain may not be used to construct future Terminators. It is this act of noble self-sacrifice that distinguishes the Terminator as a Mythic hero from the hyper-masculine Egoic heroes described earlier. Everyone waited for a sequel, which would cover humanity's battle

*Jason and the Argonauts* (1963), *The Golden Voyage of Sinbad* (1974) and *Sinbad and the Eye of the Tiger* (1977), *Clash of the Titans* (1981), all of which worked as producer or associate producer and on visual effects.

against the machine in the near future, expanding upon the brief battle scenes and evocative images of cyborgs and robot tanks crushing mounds of human skulls in the first two movies. Unfortunately, the 2003 sequel *Terminator 3: Rise of the Machines* was a poor imitation of *Terminator 2*. The 2009 *Terminator Salvation*, finally set in the future, failed to capture the evocative scenes of the war as glimpsed in the first two movies, and presented itself as nothing more than another banal Hollywood action special effects movie. Ironically, it ends in a similar fashion to *Terminator 2*, the charismatic cyborg Marcus Wright (here played by Sam Worthington, who steals the show, much as Arnold Schwarzenegger had with the first two movies) sacrificing his life to save a rather bland John Connor.

The reason for the failure of the two sequels is clear. The end of the second movie was the logical end of the story (and the mythic cycle). The future battle could never be shown because no merely human recreation could come close to the Imaginal image in the minds of fans of the franchise. As with George Lucas' disappointing *Star Wars* prequels (and the even more disappointing Disney sequels), these later movies no longer had a mythopoetic foundation to rely on and were forced to repeat themes in the earlier movies, in the end becoming no different to any other contemporary whizz bang sci-fi movies.

Similar to the transformation of Other (Shadow) to Hero (Ego Ideal) is the Shadow-Other to *Animus*-Ideal. This is shown in the transformation of the vampire myth. The traditional vampire, the male Shadow figure or monstrous Other, was originally represented by Irish author Bram Stoker's *Dracula* (in the 1897 novel of the same name), a cruel but elegant aristocrat. By the early 20th century, the

Shadow elements had resulted in misshapen or grotesque form, represented by *Nosferatu*, in the 1922 German Expressionist film directed by F. W. Murnau and starring Max Schreck as the vampire. The vampire mythos was revolutionized by American author of erotic gothic horror Ann Rice, who in the 70s and 80s transformed the vampire as Other into the vampire as a still dangerous but now *Animus* figure. The vampire has now become a decadent immortal sensualist, represented by the figure of Lestat.[97] Whereas the Nosferatu vampire Count Orlok is simply an unauthorized adaptation of Bram Stoker's Dracula (hence the change of names and other details), Lestat and his fellow vampires are authentically distinct and are as much influential on the genre as the original Dracula. The final transformation to full-blown *Animus* ideal by Stephanie Myers' Edward Cullen of *Twilight*. The *Twilight* vampires represent the defanging (literally, they don't have fangs) of the frightening Dracula/Nosferatu. The result is the romantic fantasy *Animus* figure, with the vampire as strong and vaguely menacing, but always protective, male.

An alternative take on this is the vampire not as Shadow/Other but as Profane-Egoic or even Mundane-Personal and Mythic self or companion. One of the first popular examples of this is White Wolf Gaming Studio's roleplaying game *Vampire: The Masquerade*, which first appeared in 1991 and allowed the player to take the role of a vampire as part of a larger vampire society. This was followed by further games of the series that featured werewolves and other fantastical creatures. These were eventually incorporated into a single World

---

[97] Although Rice has written many novels, probably the most important here are the first three: *Interview with the Vampire* (1976), *The Vampire Lestat* (1985), and *The Queen of the Damned* (1988).

of Darkness (or WoD) universe, featuring vampires, werewolves, mages, and more. The 2003 action-horror film *Underworld*, about a secret war between vampires and werewolves, closely copied the White Wolf games and novels, resulting in legal action against Sony Pictures and a confidential settlement.[98] More recently (2010), the surprisingly well-written (by English actor, comedian, and screenwriter Toby Whithouse) BBC 3 horror drama series *Being Human* features a vampire, a werewolf, and a female ghost as friends and flatmates. Here being a monster is not a sign of being accursed but represents alienation from everyday society. Jack Kirby and Stan Lee's *X-Men*, mutants with special powers who therefore don't fit in, are similar. Ultimately, every gnostic is an alien and an outsider,[99] often demonized and hunted by mainstream society because their unique knowledge is a threat to the *status quo* (here we might consider everything from Christian persecution of Albigensians to the fate of Islamic mystics such as Sohrawardi and Mansur al-Hallaj to the Medieval European persecution of village women and herbal healers to the American Food and Drug administration's hounding of William Reich, completely with Nazi style book burnings of his work). We, in the West, are fortunate to live in one of the few periods and civilizations in history in which people are not persecuted if their spiritual beliefs or insights

---

[98] See Collins and White Wolf v. Sony Pictures <http://www.avvo.com/case/view/collins-and-white-wolf-v—sony-pictures-11181> (Retrieved 3 June 2010, thanks to Wikipedia for bringing this to my attention). See also Fur Against Fang – Television Tropes & Idioms <http://tvtropes.org/pmwiki/pmwiki.php/Main/FurAgainstFang> for the popularity of this particular trope, with its mash up of two stock monster characters of action horror.

[99] Hans Jonas, *The Gnostic Religion: the Message of the Alien God and the Beginnings of Christianity*, Boston: Beacon Press, 2nd ed., 1963, pp.49ff.

differ from that of the ruling ideology. Even so, there will always be an Other, as long as human beings are unable to acknowledge their Shadow side.

The ultimate, cosmological-mythic Other is, however, the Apocalypse. The Apocalypse is the Other projected into cosmic time, made global and placed at the "end of history." This is itself an Egoic archetype because the Ego is terrified of its own dissolution — and the dissolution of its safe little empire — the internalized image of the mundane world it knows and interacts with. This is why the Apocalypse is such a potent archetype in Egoic mythologies (less so in Transpersonal/Mythic mythologies).

Here a distinction can be made between (a) the purely exoteric, Judaeo-Christian religious Apocalypse, (b) the apocalypse or Judgment as a metaphor for the afterlife encounter with the Higher Self,[100] (c) the esoteric hermeneutic of Apocalypse as individual gnostic transformation,[101] and (d) the collective or global

---

[100] The theme of an afterlife review occurs in Theosophy, while the Near Death account as described by Raymond Moody (*Life After Life*) features a being of Light, and is a benign spiritual experience. In the *Tibetan Book of the Dead* (*Bardo Thodel* – literally *The Great Liberation Through Hearing During The Intermediate State*) however it is a more terrifying encounter with the Lord of Death, typical of Judgment scene of most afterlife conceptions (Egyptian, Christian, Islamic, etc), although the emphasis is still placed on realizing that all experiences are none other than one's own original Consciousness or ultimate reality; in nonduality traditions such as Advaita Vedanta, Dzogchen, and Mahamudra, this realization confers Liberation.

[101] Christophoros, Apocalypse of the Soul: An Exploration of Judeo-Christian Eschatology (no longer on-line) http://singleeyemovement. com/articles-a-essays/60-christophoros/86-apocalypse-of-the-soul-an-exploration-of-judeo-christian-eschatology. Compare also the

Divinisation of the Earth as a whole, as described by Sri Aurobindo, Teilhard de Chardin, and (in secular and technological form) Transhumanism. The latter two provide a Transcendental perspective that is concerned not with mythopoesis but gnosis, while (b) represents an occult and Imaginal experience. While fully acknowledging these gnostic interpretations, I will focus on the exoteric mythos or (a) above, as this remains a powerful motif in the modern world.

The exoteric Apocalypse is represented by classical apocalyptic literature such as the *Book of Daniel, Dead Sea Scrolls*, and *Book of Revelations*, the more recent Hal Lindsey's 1970s *Late Great Planet Earth* theology, and the 16 volume "Left Behind" series of Profane/Egoic action novels by Tim LaHaye and Jerry B. Jenkins, published from the mid-nineties to mid-noughties. Christian End of Times eschatology also appears in Hollywood movies such as the *Seventh Sign* (1988), *End of Days* (1999), and *The Reaping* (2007). However, none of these attained blockbuster status (the very successful *Exorcist* and *Omen* horror franchises would probably also technically qualify here, but they are better placed under the heading of the Shadow/Other). A very different and far more profound appropriation of Christian archetypes is Swedish director Ingmar Bergman's 1957 *The Seventh Seal*. This is a mythopoetic drama that features the journey of a medieval knight (Max von Sydow) across a plague-ridden landscape and includes an iconic game of chess with Death.

---

relation between esoteric and exoteric apocalyptism and that between the inner Jihad (spiritual struggle against one's own lower nature) of Sufism and the outer Jihad of exoteric Islam. In both instances profound mystical symbolism can be found in religious scripture that on the surface refers to something quite different.

However, the influence of secular modernity has meant that religious symbolism and stories regarding the end times have given way to rationalist explanations such as nuclear war, environmental disaster, asteroid impact, and so on. In the mid-1990s, however, interest moved away from the apocalypse to a post-apocalyptic world whose demise was never explained.[102] With one exception, the Apocalypse has become increasingly irrelevant to the public imagination. In contrast, the post-apocalyptic world, as a future wild west type survivalist or adventure mythos, remains as popular as ever.

That exception is the Zombie apocalypse, which in the 90s and noughties has caught the popular geek imagination in a way that Hal Lindsey's premillennialism inspired religious believers in the 1970s and 80s. Today's pop culture zombie derives from the satirical horror movies of American director and screenwriter George Romero, beginning with 1968 *Night of the Living Dead* and *Dawn of the Dead* ten years later. Since the mid-noughties, the zombie mythos has taken off in a big way, with countless computer games, the best selling books of Max Brooks (*Zombie Survival Guide, World War Z*), and even a mash-up with Jane Austin, *Pride and Prejudice and Zombies*, which inverted the original romantic classic and has become an unexpected best-seller.[103]

---

[102] Christophoros, Apocalypse of the Soul: An Exploration of Judeo-Christian Eschatology (no longer on-line). Compare also the relation between esoteric and exoteric apocalyptism and that between the inner Jihad (spiritual struggle against one's own lower nature) of Sufism and the outer Jihad of exoteric Islam. In both instances profound mystical symbolism can be found in religious scripture that on the surface refers to something quite different.

[103] For more on this discussion see Craig Wilson, *USA Today*, Zombies lurch into popular culture via books, plays, more, 8 Apr 2009

The zombie is, like the vampire, a symbol of the Other as the Shadow. But whereas the Vampire is a skulking (or aristocratic, or romantic) yet intelligent and alluring super parasite who lives off humanity but always remains a secret minority, the zombie is a far more horrifying figure.[104] This grotesque mindless creature craves human flesh and turns anyone it touches into another zombie. Vampires have, according to the popular mythos, co-existed with humanity for centuries. Zombies constitute a sudden outbreak of undead that was originally supernatural but later iterations of the mythos attributed to a supervirus or government experiment gone wrong. This no doubt influenced by the 'Government as Other' motif (popular with conspiracy theorists). The authorities are slow to respond to the zombie problems — and when they do, they are unable to control them — so the zombies continue to multiply, leading to the entire human population being zombified.

There may be several reasons for the Profane/Egoic popularity of zombies for the mostly young, mostly male, "geek" demographic. With the romanticization and feminization of the vampire (see discussion on *Twilight*,

<http://www.usatoday.com/life/books/news/2009-04-08-zombies-pop-culture_N.htm>; Doug Gross, Why we love those rotting, hungry, putrid zombies – CNN.com 2 Oct 2009 <http://edition.cnn.com/2009/SHOWBIZ/10/02/zombie.love/index.html> Zombies in Popular Culture <http://www.squidoo.com/zombiefic>; Stefan Dziemianowicz, Might of the Living Dead – A ghoulish genre gets new life *Publishers Weekly* Volume 256 Issue 28 07/13/2009 <http://www.publishersweekly.com/pw/print/20090713/11921-might-of-the-living-dead-.html>; for just a few examples.

[104] Andrea Krantz – Vampires vs. Zombies: Why Brain-Eating is Better than Blood-Sucking, December 11th, 2008 <http://news.gotgame.com/vampires-vs-zombies-why-brain-eating-is-better-than-blood-sucking/20237/>.

sect. 20), the zombie by default becomes the most frightening representation of the Other. A world overrun by zombies and thus devoid of all meaning and purpose (other than the need to stay alive) serves as a perfect Egoic fantasy for young males who love to shoot or blow up things (there is no shortage of targets). It provides a simpler, more exciting, one-dimensional world, which can serve as a refuge from the complexities of mundane life. Thus the zombie apocalypse, which includes anything from survival-horror to the mythopoetic icon of the nerd as zombie slayer (see Edgar Wright's 2004 horror-comedy *Shaun of the Dead*), represents the Egoic hyper-masculine response to the hyper-feminine vampire's lover.

Yet ultimately, the zombie apocalypse goes nowhere. It only has two possible outcomes: either all the survivors are killed, and the whole world is zombified, or a cure is found, and humanity is saved, in which case civilization is restored. This latter ties in with the post-apocalyptic hero as the savior of civilization. Here an iconic cross-over (which precedes the modern zombie fad by many years, the creatures are probably closer to vampires) is Richard Matheson's little-known 1954 novel *I Am Legend*. I remember how powerfully influenced by youthful imagination was by Boris Sagal's 1971 cinematic adaptation *The Omega Man* (starring Charlton Heston). A recent remake is Francis Lawrence 2007 film *I Am Legend*, starring Will Smith. In both versions, the hero is a Christ-like figure whose sacrifice buys time so the precious antidote can be passed on to cure the vampire-zombie plague (representing the Other, chaos, and the dissolution of Ego) and restore civilization.

Like all profane/Egoic fiction and its associated mythoi, the zombie apocalypse provides a static scenario that lacks the dynamism of authentic Mythic story-telling with its hero's journey and motifs of initiation, transformation, and the distinction between the mundane and the magical world. Hence the exoteric apocalypse, whether religious, as in end-time theology, or secular, as in the zombie mythos,[105] must be replaced by a more dynamic evolutionary transcendence.

One of the greatest writers of the fantastical was New England Gothic horror writer Howard Phillips Lovecraft, whose imagination was inspired by his frequent nightmares. A seminal figure in the genres of both science fiction and horror, Lovecraft was one of the very few writers to portray non-anthropocentric, non-Egoic, and non-Shadow Other. Here there is an expansion from the limited personal and rational ego to an Imaginal World that transcends the mundane. Although terrifying, it is not claustrophobic or restrictive in the way that the standard repetitive narrative of the unstoppable serial killer and monster is. Instead, it represents a sort of dark gnosis, that the ordinary person will flee from, back to the safety of the ignorance of the mundane Ego and the limited understanding of science.

Relatively unknown in his lifetime, Lovecraft would go on to become one of the most influential writers of the fantastical; his influences including horror maestro Stephen King, movie directors Roger Corman, John Carpenter (*The Thing*), Ridley Scott (*Alien* franchise), and Guillermo del Toro, graphic novel writers Mike Mignola (*Hellboy*) and Alan Moore, graphic novel and fantasy author Neil Gaiman, game designer Gary Gygax

---

[105] Brief mention should be made of End-Time zombie crossover *Legion*, a 2010 American apocalyptic fantasy-horror film directed by Scott Stewart.

(*Dungeons & Dragons*), the science fiction-horror-fantasy franchise *Warhammer 40k*, and many others.

Lovecraft's Cthulhu Mythos must surely rank equally with Tolkien's Middle Earth as one of the most authentic and potent examples of mythopoesis in the 20th century. Ironically, Lovecraft was a materialist and would no doubt have been amused at the way his many admirers have interpreted his ideas in non-reductionist terms.

*Fig.12.* "The Shadow Out of Time" by H. P. Lovecraft. Painted by Howard V. Brown. *Astounding Stories* magazine, June 1936.

Lovecraft described a cosmology in which man is utterly insignificant against the vast impersonality of the cosmos and the terrifying monsters and alien races that inhabit it. His stories usually revolve around a protagonist who ventures beyond the safe boundaries of modern knowledge, finally going insane with the realization of the true nature of reality. While his stories are usually described as horror, many, such as *At the Mountains of Madness* and *The Shadow Out of Time* (illustrated), feature extraterrestrial aliens, and hence can equally be described as science fiction or horror-science fiction crossover.

## 27. EVOLUTION AND TRANSCENDENCE

Transcendence differs from the conventional Apocalypse mythos in that it is free of the grotesqueness of popular exoteric Christian-inspired mythologies. It also emphasizes the individual, although it can be collective as well.

In the old days, attempts to describe Transcendence through story-telling involved epic poetry and mythological tales of gods, and so on. Good examples are the Hindu *Mahabharata* (which includes the Bhagavad Gita, the most revered work of mystical literature in Hinduism) and the Christian Bible. All of these were presented as objective facts. Hence it was believed as literal truth (and sometimes still is) that Krishna picked up a mountain, Jesus ascended bodily to heaven, and so on. Since then, human consciousness has moved on, and religious fundamentalism is no longer credible (except to fundamentalists).

Stories of transcendence and Divinization are still found in the modern world. Sri Aurobindo sought to present his insight of the Supreme (and Divinization – the Supramental Transformation) through the medium of epic poetry, taking the old Hindu legend of *Savitri* and updating it. The result is a profound work, considered by many to be Sri Aurobindo's greatest, but, like almost all of his material, written in a heavy 19th-century style of Romanticism that makes it almost impossible for the non-devotee and non-scholar to read, especially if you don't have an aptitude for poetry.

Sri Aurobindo's teaching of Supramental Divinization finds an echo in Stanley Kubrick and Arthur C. Clarke's *2001: A Space Odyssey* (there is also a novel Clarke wrote concurrently with the film, I found it, like a lot of concept-driven science fiction, bland and dry in style). The theme of transcendence is also found in the novels of Olaf Stapledon – *Last and First Men* and *Star Maker* (or *Nebula Maker*), which date from the 1930s. Along with Russian Cosmism, Stapledon represents the beginning of the Transhumanist ideal of future evolution beyond the current limited human condition.

Here we have again the distinction between the archetypes, tropes, and motifs of traditional mythology and religion, which are orientated to the past, and the transtypes, which point to a future full of amazing posthuman and science fictional possibilities.

A similar contrast here is between the earlier, religious or spiritual evolutionary mystics, who apply premodern myths, religions, and archetypes to the posthuman future, and the more recent, ultratech inspired Transhumanists, who reject premodern thinking altogether. Spiritually orientated late 19th and early 20th century figures like Sri Aurobindo, Teilhard de Chardin, and the religious Russian Cosmists, presented various — and often exceedingly profound — approaches to the unity of premodern mythic religions of the past with the evolutionary and trans-modern promise of a future transcendence that is beyond religion. In contrast, late 20th century technophile futurists, Transhumanists, and singularitarians adopt a purely secular approach, in which transcendence is explained in terms of the rational-mental.

Transhumanists, along with science fiction writers, worldbuilders, and imagineers of the future, created and embodied entire new symbols, or transtypes, of transformation within the historical physical culture and society, and feeding back possibilities from the Imaginal future, where they interacted and interact with the established iconic Imaginal archetypes and symbols of God and the transcendent.

Of course, the physicalism of secular Transhumanism is as limiting as the pre-scientific and premodern religions of the past. However, as transcendence turns out, it is not likely to be definable in terms of modern-day categories.

Today in the early 21st century, we have visionary space entrepreneurs and billionaires like Elon Musk (SpaceX), Richard Branson (Virgin Galactic), and Jeff Bezos (Blue Origin) rather than hide-bound Governments promising a future of humanity going beyond the limits of Earth-bound civilization. Originally with space tourism, which is obviously the easiest to achieve, but soon actual colonies in orbit, on the Moon, and Mars. The mythopoetic imagination of mid-20th-century science fiction becomes the actual attainment of early 21st-century venture capitalism.

The sense of wonder and excitement at the actual attainment, not just the possibility promised by science fiction, of space expansion and colonization will alter the collective imagination forever. Symbolically, the physical transcendence of gravity and the expansion of humanity into the universe is equivalent to the old spiritualist and theosophical idea of humanity evolving to more spiritual states. Except that this is an Imaginal transtype from the future, rather than an archetype from the collective unconscious and racial memory of the premodern, pre-technological past.

As with other hard science fiction tropes, Transhumanism and Cosmic Expansionism often go together, as part of the convergence of transtypes from the Imaginal future. For example, in addition to being a space entrepreneur, Musk is also a self-proclaimed Transhumanist.[106]

Interestingly, a regressive holdover of the old dualistic Platonism, Gnosticism, and Mysticism in which the body is considered inferior, and identity resides solely with the mind or spirit, is found in the Transhumanist concept of mind uploads or emulations, where an immortal digital existence — perhaps with occasional downloads into cyborg bodies — is considered superior to the full-blooded existence in the organic body, or at the very least more practical.[107] It's easy to see how some socially and physically awkward nerds could be attracted to a virtual

---

[106] Devika Khandelwal, Ray Kurzweil and Elon Musk are self-proclaimed "Transhumanists" 2021.<https://www.logically.ai/factchecks/library/261d5366>

[107] See Mind uploading, Wikipedia <https://en.wikipedia.org/wiki/Mind_uploading> and also Transhumanism Wiki <https://transhumanism.fandom.com/wiki/Mind_uploading> for a comprehensive review. Robin Hanson, *The Age of Em: Work, Love and Life when Robots Rule the Earth*, Oxford University Press, 2016, suggests that an age of mind emulations will be a short transitional period between the modern world and the technological Singularity.

existence (although, as a nerd myself, I find the possibility of a virtual-only existence to be chilling). Yet this is the opposite not only of the transtypal Imaginal promise of human space colonization, but also the body-affirming yogic techniques of Taoist Alchemy, some elements of Tantra, and the Integral Yoga of Sri Aurobindo.

The suggestion — popular in Transhumanist science fiction, the works of West Australian hard science fiction writer Greg Egan for example, with his 1997 novel *Diaspora*, and more recently Dennis E. Taylor's popular and less rigorous Bobiverse series (*We Are Legion (We Are Bob)*, 2016, and sequels) — that mind emulation interstellar travel would be easier as it would do away with bulky life support systems, makes the highly dubious assumption that the advanced nanotech (and perhaps quantum computing) computers carrying the uploads wouldn't be highly sensitive to cosmic radiation and would be reliable over periods of centuries.

At the same time, paranoia regarding Transhumanism by backward-looking Conspiracy Theorists[108] and the anti-Space Expansionism neo-luddism of the so-called "solar punk" Left[109] represent the fear of the future and the denial of the transtypal.

---

[108] For example David Livingstone, *Transhumanism: The History of a Dangerous Idea,* Kindle Edition, 2015.

[109] I discovered to my surprise the anti-progress orientation in a Solarpunk group on Facebook in early 2021. Previously I had strongly identified with Solarpunk — see the TV Tropes definition<https://tvtropes.org/pmwiki/pmwiki.php/Main/SolarPunk> — not realising the extreme neo-luddism, tall poppy syndrome, and anti-space colonisation attitude of what I have come to refer to as the"regressive left."

There is no doubt an evolutionary, space-based humanity, however, will be the start of a new "Cambrian Explosion," as humans and other sentient beings (such as A.I., cyborgs, biological robots, and genetically-enhanced animals) evolve into many different forms and niches, in keeping with the conditions and environments they face, and the roles they play in the interplanetary (and eventually interstellar) ecologies and societies of the future.

## 28. THE IMAGINAL IN ITSELF

**B**eyond secular and religious myth-making, there is an occult, esoteric, and initiatory narrative that emphasizes the Imaginal, Noetic and Transcendent reality in itself. With the pure Imaginal, storytelling as we know it is replaced by occult and initiatory accounts. Although esotericism is based on narratives that can be appreciated on many levels, like the Sufi and Kabbalistic contrast between the external allegory or literal religious account and the secret inner meaning, very little of this actually becomes assimilated into the popular consciousness. The Imaginal, unlike the Mythic, requires going beyond Egoic wish-fulfillment and projections altogether. Rather than indirect and anthropomorphic myths and tropes, there is direct experience of the Transpersonal and non – and trans-human. The Imaginal is best communicated through mystic allegory,[110] revelatory accounts (whether traditional as in the vision of Ezekiel or Enoch), dreams, surreal art, or direct experience (e.g., the accounts of

---

[110] The gnostic *Hymn of the Pearl* and Dante's *Divine Comedy are* obvious classic examples. But many more, less well known, can also be listed, such as `Ali ibn Fazel Mazandarani's *Account of strange and marvellous things...* as elucidated by Henry Corbin ( *Mundus Imaginalis, or the Imaginary and the Imaginal,* pp.23ff.).

Robert Monroe regarding his out of body experiences.)[111] This is a fascinating subject indeed but it seems to be very difficult to portray in a fictional narrative, in which its very nature is mundanely and Egoically-based. Unlike anthropocentric and anthropomorphic, Profane-Egoic, Mundane-Personal, and Mythic storytelling which everyone can understand and appreciate, a purely Imaginal narrative would only make sense to those who already possess gnosis. Even much of gnostic revelation is itself still anthropocentric and anthropomorphic because of the inevitable effect of the distorting perspective of individual consciousness. But this is a whole new topic, which belongs to esotericism proper. Nevertheless, there are many anthropomorphic and gnostic accounts, such as the Gnostic *Hymn of the Pearl*, Dante's *Divine Comedy*, and even elements of visionary writers like science fiction author Philip K. Dick, that provide direct insight into transcendental realms. This is the reason why such narratives will always have great power to inspire and fascinate.

---

[111] Robert Monroe *Journeys Out of the Body* (1971), *Far Journeys* (1985), and *The Ultimate Journey* (1994). Monroe was an American advertising executive whose works remain among the most eloquent and profound accounts of an out of body experience, written in a manner accessible to the modern reader. Even so, some of this material reads like science fiction/fantasy and hence no doubt involves personal elements; it is very difficult to portray the Imaginal directly.

## 29. THE IMPORTANCE OF MYTHOPOESIS FOR THE MODERN WORLD

We live in a world that is more complex and disorientating than any that our ancestors experienced. A world of countless fields of specialized knowledge, complex social, political, environmental, economic issues, and existential crises where the previous threat of nuclear holocaust has been joined by new threats such as anthropogenic global warming, biodiversity crash, plastic, chemical and electromagnetic pollution, and depletion of natural resources. There is more information than ever before, so much so that we are drowning in a sea of information. Bad faith actors now regularly use social media to perpetuate misinformation and manipulate the gullible.[112]

Modernity has overthrown the worst excesses of theocratic Abrahamic religion, at least in the West, but has not provided anything to replace it with. In this rudderless world, expert knowledge is replaced by conspiracy theories and the progressive center by regressive politics

---

[112] See for example Guy Burgess and Heidi Burgess, Challenging "Bad-Faith" Actors Who Seek to Amplify and Exploit Our Conflicts, Beyond Intractability, March, 2021 <https://www.beyondintractability.org/frontiers/bad-faith-actors>. Accessed 31 May 2021.

of left and right, as people struggle to find meaning and identity in a meaningless world.

This is where mythopoesis comes in. Mythopoesis allows us to create and participate in our own story or take on elements of other stories and universes, such as fanfic and cosplay. Mythopoesis answers the absurdist meaninglessness of the material world with engagement in the hero's journey, symbols of transformation, and the fantastic landscape of the Imaginal.

While there will always, unfortunately, be narcissistic garbage in the mass media and low-grade storytelling, as referenced by Sturgeon's Law[113] — ninety percent of everything is crud — but there will also be rare works of genius that continue to inspire, uplift, and provide meaning and purpose. It is this level of transformative, Imaginal, and spiritually-infused mythopoesis that serves as a beacon of adventure in a world of everyday banality.

---

[113] American science fiction author and critic Theodore Sturgeon noted that not only is most science fiction of very low quality, but this can also be applied to other genres of writing, art, or indeed anything.

GLOSSARY


*Anima/Animus* – in Jungian psychology, that aspect of the unconscious psyche that is of the nature of the opposite gender and psychological orientation to the Ego. Projected onto others it becomes an idealized love interest, a common theme in fiction.

*Anti-Hero* – the morally ambiguous hero, a reflection of our modern age which rejects the absolutist values of the past, in favour of moral ambiguity that allows a greater depth of character development.

*Apocalypse, Post-Apocalyptic* – as here defined, a genre of mundane-egoic fiction, in which civilization has been destroyed by some fantastical threat or crisis, such as aliens, zombies, robots, war, end of fossil fuels, global warming, cosmic radiation, dragons, or some other arbitrary plot device, leaving the survivors to cope in a lawless world as best they can. A form of imaginal story-telling (albeit often of the most banal sort) in that it takes place in a world no longer our own.

*Archetype* – in Platonism, an ideal spiritual form, of which the phenomenal world is a mere imitation or copy. In Jungian psychology, primordial symbols of transformation within the Collective Unconscious. They appear spontaneously in the myths and legends of all cultures, as well as spontaneously in individual dreams, visions, the fantasies of schizophrenics, and in psychedelic drug experiences.

*Collective Unconscious* – as described by Jung, the deeper layers of the psyche that are not limited to the individual, but include cultures and races as a whole. The repository of primordial images or archetypes, which are symbols and transformation. Overlaps with and in part synonymous with the Imaginal world.

*Ego* – center of identity within the psyche, mediates between the inner (imaginal, phenomenological, unconscious) and outer (objective, empirical, quantitative) worlds. Due to the focus of psychic energy, May tend to narcissism when not balanced by a sense of perspective and self-knowledge. The personal as opposed to the Transpersonal.

*Faerie* - the world of fairy tales, myth, and Fantasy genre as an actual imaginal reality (as described in an essay by J. R. R. Tolkien).

*Fantasy* – a genre of fantastical story-telling and mythopoesis associated with Modernity, that tends to project backwards into a mundane or imaginal faux medieval European or faux barbarian past future, although there is a tendency now towards Asian, Urban, New Weird, Steampunk (faux 19th century) Fantasy as well.

*Five Man Band* – a common trope in science fiction and Fantasy, in which a team of adventurers are defined according to particular typal categories such as leader, foil, big guy, smart guy, and feeling type or healer.

*Gnosis* – imaginal, noetic, or transcendent understanding that goes beyond both the arbitrary belief and the limited reasoning of the ordinary or mundane ego. Mythopoesis often incorporates gnostic elements, even when the mythopoet him or herself is not aware of it.

*Great Chain of Being* – the series of being or realities from the highest Godhead down to base matter. A common theme in pre-modern metaphysics.

*Hero* – an idealized, larger than life, individual, who embodies the values of a particular culture, and goes through adventure, trials, and transformation. The journey and qualities of the hero has been mapped out in great detail by mythographer Joseph Campbell.

*Hypostasis* – a term adopted from Plotinus; refers to one of the perhaps arbitrary divisions of reality that underlie and precede both everyday consciousness and material nature. The series of hypostases make up the Great Chain of Being.

*Imaginal* – the universal phenomenological reality that is the subjective counterpole of the external empirical universe. The source of myth, meaning, and creative imagination. The collective unconscious, in part. In terms of the Great Chain of Being this is the reality immediately behind and above the gross physical.

*Magical consciousness* – a mode of understanding in which the universe is not distinct from the individual. Immersion in the Imaginal world.

*Modernity* – especially in Western civilization, the revolution in art, learning, and philosophy of the Renaissance, the printing press and the Protestant Revolution of the 15th and 16th centuries, the rise of merchant capitalism, and the scientific, rational, and philosophical secular revolution of the 16th, 17th, and 18th centuries. Equivalent to reason and rationality. Jean Gebser refers to this as Mental-Perspectival mutation of consciousness.

*Mundane* – the world of ordinary experience; that part of the infinite Cosmos that pertains to one's finite everyday objective physical existence; non-Fortean physical reality.

*Mundane-egoic* – the ordinary, banal, everyday consciousness and the world it relates to. Existence apart from the imaginal and the mythopoetic.

*Mundane-Personal* – storytelling intermediate between infantile Profane-Egoic narcissism and Mundane non-fiction. It is more realistic than the Profane-Egoic, but is still an invented story, rather than an empirical account about the physical world. Includes well written fiction with good character development, realistic situations, and a much greater degree of verisimilitude to Profane-Egoic stories and daydreams.

*Myth, Mythic* – a mode of transpersonal, imaginal, understanding and explaining the world in which the imaginal and symbolic is projected anthropomorphically onto the banal everyday reality, usually in the form of larger than life legends and stories.

*Mythopoesis* – the act and art of creating myths; articulating the Imaginal for current world or society.

*Nous, Noetic* – the hypostasis intermediate between the Psychic and the Absolute. Pure consciousness, cosmic transpersonal archetypes.

*Other, the* – psychic, numinous, imaginal form for any person or group distinct from one's own self or ingroup. Usually possessing an alien or uncanny aspect, may be a vehicle of the Shadow.

*Personal* – pertaining to aspects of consciousness or of the psyche that pertain to the individual self or the Ego.

*Pre-modern* – magical and mythical thinking, religious literalism, nostalgia for a mythic past, pertaining to culture, society, psychology, and worldview prior to the rise of Modernity (q.v.).

*Profane-Egoic* – the lower, narcissistic subjective imagination of the ego-personality, without input from the transpersonal, Imaginal, archetypal, transtypal, or from any higher spiritual dimensions. Involves daydreams and wish-fulfillment fantasies projected on the Mundane objective world of actual physical experience.

*Profane or egoic imagination* – story-telling imagination limited to the perspective of the ego, and not incorporating imaginal and mythic elements.

*Psychic* – also "Soul", subjectivity, inner life, the hypostasis intermediate between the material reality and the Noetic. sometimes equated with the Imaginal, and sometimes intermediate between the Imaginal and the Noetic.

*Psychic Being* – in Sri Aurobindo's Integral Psychology, the evolving, reincarnating Divine essence or Soul, which is the template for, and projected outwards as, the Jungian archetype of Self.

*Psychotype* – a personality type, as illustrated in pre-modern myths. Polytheism as psychology. Commonly but incorrectly identified with Jungian archetypes.

*Rational/Mundane polarity* – ordinary consciousness, orientated to the external world of everyday experience, as opposed to the often irrational, inner, imaginal world. Equivalent to Gebser's Mental-Perspectival.

*Retrocausality* – causality that moves backwards in time, such as events from the future influencing the present.

*Sacred* – Divine, transpersonal, or imaginal object, reality, or story, which is infused with meaning. Pertaining to religion as a representative of the pre-modern imaginal. The opposite of mundane or profane.

*Science Fiction* – a broad genre of fantastical story-telling and mythopoesis associated with Modernity, that tends to project forward into a mundane or imaginal future, rather than dwell nostalgically on a mythical past.

*Self* – in Jungian psychology, the center around which the entire psyche revolves. Being unconscious, it is the counterpole and opposite to the Ego. The Self appears in culture and psychology as the projected or idealized God-image; for example Christ or Buddha.

*Shadow* – in Jungian psychology, the repressed contents of the psyche, which tend to be projected onto the world or onto other individuals and groups as a scapegoat or personification of all evil.

*Space Expansionism* – future-imaginal possibility and promise of humanity's expansion beyond the Earth, and the colonization of the universe.

*Space Opera* – a subgenre of science fiction that emphasizes melodramatic, over the top story and characters at the expense of realism, tends to entertainment rather than intelligent speculation. Has a strong resemblance to pre-modern myths, the difference being it is set in an imaginal future rather than an imaginal past.

*Story-telling* – the art of weaving a story, whether in text, comic or graphic story, animation, video game, or live action movie or T.V. form. The best story-telling is always a form of mythopoesis, because every good story is also a renewal, recreation, or creation of an imaginal myth, whether pertaining to the past, present, future, or an alternative reality.

*Superhero* – a super-powered human with god-like powers, equivalent to the heroes and deities of the pantheon of Classical Antiquity.

*Transhumanism* – philosophical movement or ideology which advocates future-imaginal (transtypal) possibilities such as human enhancement, genetic engineering, cyborgisation, artificial intelligence, and space exploration.

*Transpersonal* – pertaining to aspects of consciousness or of the psyche that totally go beyond the boundaries of the personal self or ego. Transpersonal psychology is dedicated to this larger aspect of the psyche, in contrast to conventional psychology which focuses on the individual.

*Transtype* – an imaginal form or potential with the opposite time polarity to an archetype; projecting back from a yet to physically realized imaginal motif, symbol, or power of transformation; the innovative creative power of the future.

*Trope* – a recurring theme, element, or building block of a story. Unlike archetypes, tropes are culturally determined. However, there is no sharp demarcation between the two categories.

*Worldbuilding* – the creation of an imaginary or fictional world, with its own culture, races, history, geography, plant and animal life, language, politics, and more. An essential element of all thoughtful science fiction and fantasy literature.

# INDEX

## Z

CPSIA information can be obtained
at www.ICGtesting.com
Printed in the USA
LVHW090359140322
713388LV00004B/80